GOLDEN HOURS

GOLDEN HOURS

Heart-Hymns of the Christian Life

Elizabeth Payson Prentiss

Author of *Stepping Heavenward*

SOLID GROUND CHRISTIAN BOOKS

PO Box 660132 ~ Vestavia Hills, AL 35266

SOLID GROUND CHRISTIAN BOOKS
PO Box 660132, Vestavia Hills, AL 35266
(205) 978-9469
solid-ground-books@juno.com
http://solid-ground-books.com

Golden Hours: Heart-Hymns of the Christian Life
Elizabeth Payson Prentiss (1818-1878)

Published by Solid Ground Christian Books
Copyright 2001, Solid Ground Christian Books
All rights reserved

Special thanks to Mr. Don King and the Maine Historical
Society for their help in sharing the treasures of Mrs. Prentiss.

ISBN: 0-9710169-3-3

Cover: Anthony Rotolo Design

Manufactured in the United States of America
1 2 3 4 5 6 7 8 9 10   01 02 03 04 05

Special Dedication

This book, written by a gracious sufferer of a former day,
is dedicated to a gracious sufferer in the present day:

Perpetua Cortez

In her honor the typeface, Perpetua, has been used for each title.

> *"Come unto me, my kindred! I enfold you*
> *In an embrace to sufferers only known,*
> *Close to this heart I tenderly will hold you,*
> *Suppress no sigh, keep back no tear, no groan."*
> -Elizabeth Prentiss, p. 51

~~~

"For God is not unjust so as to forget your work
and the love which you have shown toward His name,
in having ministered and in still ministering to the saints."
-Hebrews 6:10

PREFACE

Elizabeth Payson Prentiss (1818-1878) was privileged to be born into a family where love to God and to each other was the daily atmosphere of the home. She was called by God to be a life-long sufferer and thus from an early age was able to touch the hearts of the brokenhearted. It is a privilege to be able to introduce her "spiritual auto-biography" in verse, written during the most important 20 years of her life, from the death of her two children Eddie and Bessie, until the time she was being prepared for her eternal abode in glory.

She is best known for two products of her pen and her heart: the book *Stepping Heavenward,* and the hymn *More Love to Thee, O Christ.* That hymn is an apt descrip-tion of the longing of her heart: *to love Christ more deeply.* This same spirit runs through every page of this precious book of her hymns and spiritual songs of the Christian life.

Golden Hours has not been available for over 100 years. Originally published in 1873 it was used to lift the spirits of thousands on both sides of the Atlantic. It is not a book to be read through quickly, but one that must be read slowly and prayerfully. It may be helpful to include in this Preface the description that is given of this book in *The Life and Letters of Elizabeth Prentiss,* that is now available by Calvary Press Publishing under the title of her most famous hymn. Her husband, Rev. George L. Prentiss, begins his discussion of this book by quoting a letter from his wife to Mrs. Henry B. Smith, a dear friend, whose husband, a justly famous theologian, lay very sick:

"I am glad you find anything to like in my poor little book. I hear very little about it, but its publication has brought a blessing to my soul, which shows that I did right in thus making known my testimony for Christ. My will in the matter was quite overturned."

The "poor little book" appeared under the title of *Religious Poems,* afterwards changed to *Golden Hours: Hymns and Songs of the Christian Life*-- In a letter of Mrs. Prentiss to a friend, written in 1870, occurs this passage : "Most of my verses are too much my own personal experience to be put in print now. After I am dead I hope they may serve as language for some other hearts. After I am dead! That means, oh ravishing thought! that I shall be in heaven one day."

Until the fall of 1873 her husband and two or three friends only knew of the existence of these verses, and their publication had not crossed her mind. But shortly after her return from their summer home in Dorset, VT she was persuaded to let Mr. Randolph (her publisher) read them. She soon received from him the following letter:

"The poems *must* be printed, and at once! We, that is, the firm living at Yonkers, read aloud all the pieces, except those in the book, at one sitting, and would have gone on to the end but that the eyes gave out. Out of the lot three or four pieces were laid aside as not up to the standard of the others. The female member of the firm said that Mrs. Prentiss would do a wrong if she withheld the poems from the public. This member said *he* should give up writing, or trying to write, religious verses.

I am not joking. The book must be printed. We were charmed with the poems. Some of them have all the quaintness of Herbert, some the simple subjective fervor of the German hymns, and some the glow of Wesley. They are, as Mrs. R. said, out of the beaten way, *and all true.* So they differ from the conventional poetry. If published, there may be here and there some sentimental soul, or some soul without sentiment, or some critic who dotes on Robert Browning and don't understand him, or on Morris, or Rossetti, because they are high artists, who may snub the book. Very well; for compensation you will have the fact that the poems will win for you a living place in the hearts of thousands, in a sanctuary where few are permitted to enter."

A day or two later Mr. Randolph wrote in reply to her misgivings:

"If I had the slightest thought that you would make even a slight mistake in publishing, I would say so. As I have already said, I am *sure* that the book would prove a blessing in ten thousand ways, and at the same time add to your reputation as a writer."

She could not resist this appeal. The assurance that the verses would prove a blessing to many souls disarmed her scruples and she consented to their publication. The most of them, unfortunately, bore no date. But all, or nearly all of them, belong to the previous twenty years, and they depict some of the deepest experiences of her Christian life during that period; they are her tears of joy or of sorrow, her cries of anguish, and her songs of love and triumph. Some of them were hastily written in pencil, upon torn scraps of paper, as if she were on a journey. Were they all accompanied with the exact time and circumstances of their composition, they would form, in connection with others unpublished, her spiritual autobiography from the death of Eddy and Bessie, in 1852, (see Appendix Two, pp. 122-131) to the autumn of 1873.

As she anticipated, the volume met in some quarters with anything but a cordial reception; the criticisms upon it were curt and depreciatory. Its representation of the Christian life was censured as gloomy and false. It was even intimated that in her expressions of pain and sorrow, there was more or less poetical affectation. Alluding to this in a letter to a friend, she writes:

"I have spoken of the deepest, sorest pain; not of trials, but of sorrow, not of discomfort, but of suffering. And all I have spoken of, I have felt. Never could I have known Christ, had I not had large experience of Him as a Chastiser. You little know the long story of my life, nor is it necessary that you should; but you must take my word for it that if I do not know what suffering means, there is not a soul on earth that does. It has not been my habit to say much about this; it has been a matter between myself and my God; but the *results* I have told, that He may be glorified and that others may be led to Him as the Fountain of life and of light. I refer, of course, to the book of verses; I never called them poems. You may depend upon it the world is brimful of pain in some shape or other; it is a "*hurt* world." But no Christian should go about groaning and weeping; though sorrowing, he should be always rejoicing. During twenty years of my life my kind and wise Physician was preparing me, by many bitter remedies, for the work I was to do; I can never thank or love Him enough for His unflinching discipline."

Referring to the book in a letter to a friend, written shortly after its publication, she says: "Of course it will meet with rough treatment in some quarters, as indeed it has already done. I doubt if anyone works very hard for Christ who does not have to be misunderstood and perhaps mocked."

Even the favorable notices of the volume, with two or three exceptions; evinced little sympathy with its spirit, or appreciation of its literary merits. But while failing to make any public impression, the little book soon found its way into thousands of closets and sick-rooms and houses of mourning, carrying a blessing with it. Touching and grateful testimonies to this effect came from the East and the farthest West and from beyond the sea. The following is an extract from a letter to Mr. Randolph, written by a lady of New York eminent for her social influence and Christian character:

"The book of heart-hymns is wonderful, as I expected from the specimens which you read to me from the little scraps of paper from your desk. Do you know that I *lived* on them ("The School" and "My Expectation is from Thee") and was greedy to get the book that I might read them again and again. And behold, the volume is full of the things I have felt so often, *expressed* as no one ever expressed them before. I am overwhelmed every time I read it. My husband and children have quite laughed at "Mamma's enthusiasm" over a book of poems, as I am considered very prosaic. I made him read two or three of them and he *surrenders*. Our daughter, too, who is full of appreciation of poetry as well as of the *best things,* is equally delighted. I carried the volume to a sick friend and read to her out of it. I wish you could have seen how she was comforted! I do not know Mrs. Prentiss, but if you ever get a chance, I would like you to tell her what she has done for me."

One of the best notices appeared in The Churchman, an Episcopal newspaper then published at Hartford, but since transferred to New York. Here is a part of it :

"For purity of thought, earnestness and spirituality of feeling, and smoothness of diction, they are all, without exception, good -if they are not great. If no one rises to the height which other poets have occasionally reached, they are, nevertheless, always free from those defects which sometimes mar the perfectness of far greater productions. Each portrays some human thirst or longing, and so touches the heart of every thoughtful reader. There is a sweetness running through them all which comes from another than earthly source, and which human wisdom can neither produce nor enjoy."

A highly cultivated Swiss lady wrote from Geneva: "What a precious, precious book! and what mercy in God to enable us to understand, and say Amen from the heart to every line! It was He who caused you to send me a book I so much needed; and I thank Him as much as you."
(*More Love to Thee,* Calvary Press, pp. 422-425)

It is hoped that many such testimonies will once again come from far and wide to the usefulness of this little book. It is a kind providence that has permitted Solid Ground Books to publish a book by Edward Payson (*Legacy of a Legend)* at the same time as his daughter Elizabeth. They both lived to love Christ and to bring others to love Him. May they both again be used to help the weak, comfort the troubled and strengthen the hands that hang down by pointing them to the only source of help, comfort and strength, the Lord Jesus Christ.

The Publisher
August 2001

Contents

GOLDEN HOURS

Heart-Hymns of the Christian Life

"The testimony of one soul is the
experience of thousands;" --

for

"As in water face answereth to face,
so the heart of man to man."

My Golden Hours

My golden hours! My golden hours!
    O what and whence, are they?
Have they sprung up mid life's fair flowers,
    Fruits of a sun lit day?

Have I sailed forth on prosperous seas,
    Bound for the blessed land
Where I could take them at my ease,
    From off a sparkling strand?

Not so! They grew mid brambles rude,
    Sprang up mid briar and thorn,
Mid darkest nights, in solitude,
    My golden hours were born.

On stormy seas the bark was lost
    That sought these treasures rare;
I found them on a rock-bound coast;
    I plucked them from despair.

Now God be praised, who briar and thorn
    Strewed thickly on my way;
My pier-ced soul, all rent and torn,
    Shall anthems sing for aye.

And blessed be His name, who walked
    Upon life's troubled sea;
Whispered of His own peace, and talked
    As a dear Friend to me.

For in my griefs and pains and sighs,
    Mid chilling frosts and showers,
I won from my dear Lord the prize;
    His golden, golden hours!

The Battle of Life

The wintry storm was raging loud without,
    And to and fro,
The angry winds flung carelessly about,
    The falling snow.

Luxuriously before the ruddy fire
    I sat at ease,
The only object of my heart's desire
    Myself to please.

A voice aroused me from my idle dreams,
    "Rise, rise, my child!
Shake thyself loose from these unfruitful schemes,
    These fancies wild.

Come forth with me, and buffet wind and storm
    And icy cold;
Come as thou art, nor stay thy shrinking form
    Thus to enfold!"

It was the Master's voice. I could but yield
    To its behest,
While dread repugnance lay but ill concealed
    Within my breast.

Behind me closed my sheltering door; I faced
    The tempest rude;
Wild, savage winds my shrinking form embraced
    While thus I stood

Upon the threshold, casting longing eyes
    Back to my home,
Reluctant from my childhood's Paradise
    Enforced to roam.

Then plunging onward towards th' appointed way,
    I madly went,

And night and day, yea, many a night and day,
  My figure bent

Beneath the blast. Assailed with shuddering dire,
  By fears oppressed,
Despairing, hopeless, stript of all desire,
  I onward pressed.

Until I heard above the thunder's roll
  The Master's voice
Arise once more. It cried, "Oh, faithless soul,
  Behold thy choice!

A life-long childhood, basking idly on
  The lap of ease,
Or manhood's strength by long endurance won
  In toils like these.

Whether to gird thyself to walk with Me
  Mid conflicts dread,
Or back effeminate to ease to flee—
  Living—yet dead."

Already by my labors stronger grown,
  I stood and cried:
"Master and Lord! With Thee, with Thee alone,
  Let me abide.

Let me but know I buffet wind and storm,
  With Thee, with Thee!
Upon my path Thine own divinest form
  But let me see!"

Thus in the hour of battle choice was made!
  Choice of unrest!
Thus Christian manhood seeking, undismayed
  The storm I breast.

No leisure now, no dreams, no idle time;
  I wrestle on;

Beat, icy winds, oppose, oh adverse clime,
    Till victory's won.

For I shall win! I shall come forth at last
    Not lost, but found!
A Christian warrior whom each stormy blast
    Hath victor crowned!

Thanksgiving

I thank Thee, O my God, that through Thy grace
    I know Thee, who Thou art;
That I have seen the beauty of Thy face
    And felt Thee in my heart.

I thank Thee, O my Savior, who hast deigned
    To stoop to even me;
Within my inmost soul hast ruled and reigned,
    And will my ransom be.

I thank Thee, Holy Spirit, that Thy wings
    Brood o'er my wandering mind;
Bringing to my remembrance sacred things
    To which my eyes were blind.

I thank Thee, Triune God! But oh, how cold
    The warmest words I speak;
For love and goodness strange and manifold,
    All human words are weak.

O teach me, then, to praise Thee with my life,
    With stern obedience;
To make the atmosphere about me rife
    With silent eloquence!

The Gladness of My Joy
Thou art "the gladness of my joy."

The world has varied charms, yet none
    Without some base alloy,
I turn from it to Thee, my God,
    The gladness of my joy.

Sorrow may sorely press me down,
    Yet not my peace destroy,
It only drives my soul to Thee,
    Still gladness of my joy.

Earth's highest prize becomes a straw,
    A worthless, glittering toy,
Beside Thy beauty, O my God,
    The gladness of my joy.

Then let me all my heart and soul,
    My every power employ,
In serving, praising Thee, who art
    The gladness of my joy.

The Gift

I asked of Thee a gift, Jesus, my Lord,
    And my expectant eyes looked up, to see
That blessing speedily from Thy dear Hand
    Come down to me.

I waited, but it came not; asked again,
    And thought to see it come in angel-guise,
And when it lingered, found no words to tell
    My sad surprise.

Dear Savior, have I asked amiss, I cried,
    What was there lacking in my earnest prayer
Did it seek heaven upon too weak a faith
    To enter there?

Full long I pondered, hoping that the gift
 For which I earnestly my Lord besought,
Would, if attained, fill my whole soul with love,
  And holy thought.

But as He still denied it, did not choose
 To give it me, I cast and threw my will
Down at His feet, and bid it there to lie,
  Patient and still.

Should not the Hand so bountiful to me,
 Reserve the right to choose for me my good,
Should I not glory in His ways, if they
  Were understood?

Thus musing, to my closet yet once more
 I stole, if only lovingly to say,
Do what Thou wilt, dear Lord, for Thy "sweet will,"
  Is mine, alway.

When lo, within that closet, waiting me,
 I found the risen Christ, and oh what grace,
What love, what beauty and what tenderness,
  Shone in His face!

And thus He spake, "That was but seeming good,
 Thy childish ignorance so boldly craved,
Withholding it My love protected thee,
  From danger saved.

But I have come instead; yes, here am I,
 Thy longed-for Savior; lean upon my breast,
Thy disappointment shall give place to joy,
  To peace and rest!"

Ah Lord! Too sacred was that wondrous hour!
 The veil that hides it let no mortal lift;
Great was the grace I sought, but oh how small
  Beside Thy gift!

Christ Victorious

Oh, days of sickness, grief and pain,
What bring ye in your mournful train?
Gray hairs, old age before its time—
The breaking down of manhood's prime,
The trembling hand, the fainting heart,
Bruises and wounds to throb and smart,
The nerve unstrung, the sleepless brain;
Oh, these come boldly in your train.

But days of sickness, grief and pain,
Do these alone make up your train?
Not so! Not so! The ranks between
Submission's gracious form is seen;
And with the boldest of the band
Sweet Patience ventures hand in hand,
While Faith, Christ's honor to maintain
Rides, dauntless, mid your hostile train.

Come, then, wild troop of griefs and pains
And riot on my Lord's domains!
Where you lay waste, another Hand
A firmer fabric long has planned;
What you destroy, Faith's radiant smile
Declares is for a little while;
And Christ Himself shall come to reign
Victorious o'er your helpless train.

The Way Home

A stranger in a foreign land, bewildered and astray,
I sought a guide sagacious to point me out the way—
    The nearest way home.

    My hand in his enclasping,
    he led me by his side,
    Through thickets and through brambles,

into a desert wide,
A weary way home!

Other pilgrims thronged the path,
but not one of them I knew,
They eyed me with suspicion,
or with greetings cold and few;
Ah, lonely way home!

Despondent sank my heart, weary grew my toiling brain,
In the throng and in the darkness I strained my eyes in vain
To see the way home.

At last the silence breaking, "Are we almost there?" I cried;
"I am weary, breathless, lonely, yet we wander far and wide
From my own dear home!"

Then gently on my ear fell the answer grave and sweet,
"The way thou art traversing bears the print of thousand feet
By me guided home.

On these rocks they well-nigh slipped,
On these sands were parched and faint;
Every mountain pass has echoed
to the sound of their complaint,
On the hard way home.

Few were the faithful hearts
that their guide distrusted not,
That held their peace, pressed onward,
and the lonely way forgot,
In the blissful thought of home.

But when the blessed vision, through Him at last attained,
Broke on their longing sight as the mountain-top was gained,
And they saw the lost home,

Every one, straightway forgetting
all the perils, all the fears,
All the struggles, faintings,

conflicts of the fast-receding years
Kissed the hand that led home!"

He spoke, and with a smile of tenderness and love,
He raised his hand and pointed to the sunny heights above,
And I saw, I saw home!

Then with mingled joy and shame,
with contrition sad and sweet,
Bathed with tears repentant
those travel-wounded feet,
That led me to my home.

And patient now press onward, the stony path ascend,
Every hour drawing nearer to the painful journey's end—
Almost home! Almost home!

Christ Everywhere

To Zion's gates, where holy hearts are meeting,
My eager footsteps thankfully repair;
My soul, expectant, waits a joyful greeting,
For Christ, Himself, is there.

Unto my closet gladly I betake me,
Driven by sorrow, weariness and care;
Ah, what a blessed suppliant they make me,
For Christ, my Lord, is there.

Sickrooms, and broken hearts, and dying pillows,
With mournful voices fill the silent air;
Thither I go, for walking on life's billows,
The risen Christ is there.

And every day I hasten to my calling,
Facing, with fearless heart, temptation's snare;
The world's enticements cease to be appealing,
Since Christ is always there.

And so, when life's brief daylight hours are ending,
And Death, defiant, urges to despair,
Strong in immortal hope, my soul ascending,
Shall answer, Christ is there!

The Perfect Friend

Lord, from myself, my faults, my sins
    Heartsick, to Thee I flee!
With each new day anew begins
    Folly's supremacy.

And from my dearest friends I fly—
    They err, they change, they fail;
My hopes they disappoint; well-nigh
    My faith in man assail.

To Thee I come! *Thou* canst not sin;
    I come to Thee for rest!
Oh, let a weary wanderer in,
    By sin and grief opprest!

Looking to Thee, Lord, day by day,
    Let me myself forget,
Meekly content to let Thee pay,
    Dear Lord, of sin my debt.

Looking to Thee with all the love
    Once to earth's treasures given,
Content to find, at last, above,
    Perfected friends in heaven!

Christ's Invitation

Press close, my child, to Me,
    Closer to Me;
Earth hath no resting place

Ready for thee!
Straight to my shelter flee,
Press close, my child, to Me,
Closer to Me!

Love, pleasure, riches, fame,
All may be thine,
And the immortal soul
Still will repine;
I must be all to thee,
Press close, my child, to Me,
Closer to Me.

Life may for thee contend,
Hard toil and care
Strive to divide from Me,
Crowd everywhere;
Let them my servants be—
Press thee, my child, to Me,
Closer to Me.

Grief of thy heart may make
A desert drear,
Yet there My suff'rers learn
My voice to hear,
Calling, with earnest plea,
Press close, my child, to Me,
Closer to Me.

Come, then, my child to Me,
Make thyself Mine;
I give Myself to thee,
I will be Thine.
Joy, grief and care shall be
Thus binding thee to Me,
Closer to Me.

A Prayer

Oh, Strongest of the strong! Be Thou the stay
Of the weak creature that Thy hand has made;
I am so helpless that each moment brings
Some new, some pressing reason for Thine aid.

Oh, Wisest of the wise! I nothing know,
I am so ignorant, so poor, so blind!
Be Thou my Teacher, be my Light, my Guide,
Show me the pathway that I cannot find.

Oh, Thou Kindest of the kind! I come to Thee
Longing for favors that I sorely need;
Open Thy bounteous hand, for Thou art He
Whose choice it is to give, in word and deed.

Oh, Truest of the true! When others fail,
Thy years remain the same; be it my lot
To share Thy faithful friendship! Dearest Lord,
Mid human changes, oh, forget me not!

Oh, Gentlest of the gentle! Speak one word
And give one smile, one single smile to me;
No voice is soft as Thine, no earthly smile
So beautiful, so ravishing can be.

Oh, Best among the good! Make me like Thee!
Strong, wise, and kind in attributes divine,
True, gentle, good, in grace not of earth—
Let me in Thy reflected beauty shine.

God Knows

Thou knowest them that trust in Thee!
          What precious words, O Lord, are these!
Here let Thy suffering children flee,
          When struggling mid life's mysteries.

For to our childish minds, Thy will
    Looks oft times hard, and passing strange;
Loving, we doubt and fear Thee still,
    And long Thy wondrous ways to change.

Not thus we cry, would we assail
    That saintly soul with blow on blow;
Not thus should Sorrow, stern and pale,
    Put forth her hand and lay him low.

What needs he, Lord, of pain and smart?
    To Thee is he not consecrate?
His joy, his hope, his all, Thou art,
    Ever on Thee he loves to wait.

Ah, dearest Lord, Thou knowest best!
    Thou knowest them that trust in Thee!
Blessed the soul, yea, doubly blest,
    When Thou dost try its constancy.

Upon the soft and crumbling stone,
    The sculptor spends a passing hour;
He strikes immortal blows alone
    When chiseled marble feels his power.

And when the ore is rich and rare
    The miner strikes and strikes again;
Labor and toil he need not spare,
    He never can exhaust the vein.

Thou knowest, Lord, a stone to choose—
    Worthy the labor of Thy hand;
Thou fearest not the tool to use
    That gives it shape at Thy command.

Thou knowest many a hidden mine
    Where Thou canst enter at Thy will;
Treasures of faith therein are thine,
    Worthy of e'en the Master's skill.

Ah, Lord! we will not stay Thy hand
    With folly's questions, folly's fears;
Thy ways we cannot understand—
    Forgive our weakness and our tears.

Move on in Thy mysterious way,
    We'll stand aside Thy work to see;
Faithful the work, and blessed they,
    Who cannot trace, but trust in Thee.

A Song to Christ

As on a vast, eternal shore,
    The waves unceasing roll,
So He whom all the worlds adore
    Blesses thy soul, oh child of earth,
    Blesses thy human soul.

Then roll thou back in tidal waves
    Thanksgivings to His name;
Sing Christ, sing Christ, who loves and saves,
    Who built thy mortal frame, my soul,
    Who built thy mortal frame.

Day follows day, night follows night;
    And ever on their wings
Christ sends thee joy and peace and light;
    Each hour new blessings brings, my heart,
    Each hour new blessings brings.

Then let each day become a song,
    And every night a hymn;
Each hour the song, the hymn prolong,
    Till tears thine eyes bedim, thrice blest!
    Till tears thine eyes bedim.

Count up thy mercies, child of clay—
    Recount them o'er and o'er;
Yet canst thou tell, in life's short day,

The sands upon the shore, oh child?
The sands upon the shore?

Nay, then, but thou in heaven shalt sing,
Sing songs to Christ for aye;
Exultant shall thy praises ring
Through an eternal day, glad heart,
Through an eternal day!

The Bitter Cup

"The cup that my father has given me, shall I not drink it?"

I take the cup, my Father, from Thy hand;
Its every drop was measured out by Thee;
How to bring healing Thou dost understand,
Who only knowest my soul's malady.
Quick, let me drink this draught at Thy behest,
Drink it for speedy healing, speedy rest.

Nay then, Thou will'st not so! But sip by sip
Must I its bitterness disheartened taste;
To-day, to-morrow, press it to my lip,
Careful that not a single drop I waste;
And while my human soul for cordial begs,
Must drink this draught revolting to its dregs.

What then? Shall I, who go to drink with Thee,
New wine in the dear Kingdom of Thy Son,
Shrink from the cup this life holds out to me,
Asking, with coward heart, a sweeter one?
Have I not owned myself diseased and faint,
And of my poor soul-sickness made complaint?

Give me the cup, my Master! See me clasp
With willing hands, this remedy from Thine!
Forgive the mortal shudder, mortal gasp
That proves me human, proves me not divine.
Slowly each drop I'll taste, and one by one;
For Thee I drink, Lord, let Thy will be done!

Life's Promises

Oh human life, thy promises are sweet,
They fall upon the ear
In cadence charming, and their tones repeat
In accents clear.

But dost thou keep thy promise? Can I trust
Thy silvery voice,
Will it awaken echo-tones that must
Bid me rejoice?

Ah no! one voice alone my soul hath heard
That ne'er deceived,
One Heart alone the depths of mine has stirred,
Yet never grieved.

Jesus, I turn to Thee! oh let me hide
Within thy breast,
Refuge and shelter, peace and grace provide,
And needed rest.

For in the mazes of a troublous hour
I make my way;
Oh come to me, Thou hast the will, the power,
Be mine alway!

More Love to Thee, O Christ

More love to Thee, O Christ,
More love to Thee!
Hear Thou the prayer I make,
On bended knee:
This is my earnest plea
More love, O Christ, to Thee,
More love to Thee!
More love to Thee!

Once earthly joy I craved,
  Sought peace and rest,
Now Thee alone I seek,
  Give what is best:
This all my prayer shall be—
More love, O Christ, to Thee,
  More love to Thee!
  More love to Thee!

Let sorrow do its work,
  Send grief and pain,
Sweet are Thy messengers,
  Sweet their refrain,
When they can sing with me—
More love, O Christ, to Thee,
  More love to Thee!
  More love to Thee!

Then shall my latest breath
  Whisper Thy praise,
This be the parting cry
  My heart shall raise:
This still its prayer shall be—
More love, O Christ, to Thee,
  More love to Thee!
  More love to Thee!

To Be Like Thee

Oh Jesus Christ, in self-despair
I come to Thee! Hear Thou the prayer
Laid at Thy feet; I leave it there—
  To be like Thee!

Turn out the darling bosom sin,
The love of self that rules within,
My earnest longing let me win—
  To be like Thee!

O let me see Thy lovely face,
O let me hear Thy words of grace,
In Thine own image grow apace—
    To be like Thee!

O Gentle, Sinless, Undefiled,
Ev'n in Thy Justice meek and mild,
Help me, Thy loving, longing child—
    To be like Thee!

Choose

Now choose my heart!
From Jesus wilt thou part?
Because an earthly friend
Would thee attend?

What can earth give
That will untarnished live?
Hast thou found any rest
Save on Christ's breast?

Think of the price
The precious sacrifice
That Jesus paid for thee,
And to Him flee.

Thou dost still wait?
Dost dare to hesitate?
Lord Jesus makes this heart
From idols part.

Hanging on Thee
From all else let it flee,
Before Thee let it fall
Its All in All.

No Idle Wing

Oh do not let a single day go by
  On idle wings, without some loving word,
Some loving deed, from my blest heart, for Thee,
  Who art my Savior, art my risen Lord!
For Thou for me hast all things done and said;
  Hast paid my debts, hast intercession made,
When crushed with sense of weakness and of sin,
  To plead my cause with Thee I was afraid.

I know not why, I dare not ask Thee why,
  Thou hast been pleased to give such gifts to me;
It was the outgrowth of no grace of mine,
  For I had naught but sins to offer Thee.
Sins? Ah, there are not words enough to tell
  How complicate, how manifold were they!
How long I tried Thy patience, and how far
  My restless footsteps led from Thee astray.

But Thou hast lured me back, and lo I come,
  Longing to do Thy will! oh make it plain,
And let my grateful life flow forth in waves
  That shall bear many a treasure to the main.
Bear them, yet know it not, as the deep sea,
  Wots not what riches float upon its breast,
Content to ebb and flow beneath Thine eye,
  To ebb and flow simply at Thy behest.

A Feeble Prayer

Lord, I am weary of myself,
      Let me more weary be,
Stay not Thy hand until I learn
      From it for aye to flee,
And all that I have loved, to pour
      In lavish floods, on Thee.

Do not I leap for joy, when saints
    To praise Thy name combine?
Is not Thy name a sweeter sound
    Than this poor name of mine?
Do I love better to be praised
    Than to hear praise of Thine?

Alas! two passions strong and deep,
    Contend my soul within,
I love myself, but I love Thee,
    And long Thy grace to win,
Long to be like Thee, to get free
    From the old life of sin.

Which of the twain shall win the day?
    Oh empty out this heart,
Dwell there in peace and leave not self
    In its remotest part—
I want to yield it all to Thee
    Who its dear Master art.

I want to be all eye, all ear,
    Jesus, for Thee alone,
To be forgotten, lost, cast out,
    Knowing, but all unknown,
To feel Thee sitting as my King
    On undisputed throne.

This is my feeble prayer, oh hear
    My poor, my childish cry,
Do for me what I cannot do,
    And pass in mercy by.
I have not courage self to slay,
    Do Thou then make it die.

Come Home !

"My suffering child! Thy days of grief are o'er,
Come home to Me, and rest forevermore."

Jesus! Thou Lord of all! I dare not go;
No work well done for Thee I have to show.

"Great deeds I ask not; but some act of love,
One word for Me thy righteousness may prove."

Alas! I do remember no such word,
Nor one such act! Pardon me, oh my Lord!

"Yet come, my child, 'tis I who bid thee come,
Nothing I ask from thee; come home, come home."

I cannot, dare not! Call me not Thy child,
Behold my hands, my heart, with sin defiled!
Behold my wasted life, my barren years,
Behold my murmurs, my rebellious tears;
See how myself I love while cold towards thee,
My conscience seared, my hardened heart, oh see.

"I see. And since thou naught hast done for Me,
I have done all, poor, sorrowing soul, for thee;
The word that thou for Me hast never spoken,
That word I spake for thee with faith unbroken;
The loving deed thou didst not, I have done,
And interceded for thee near the throne.
Thy sins, thy wasted life, thy heart defiled,
Better I know than thou dost know them, child,
And freely all that sin I have forgiven;
Come home, my child,
                    come home to Me and heaven."

My blessed Lord! My Savior and my All!
Weeping no longer, I obey Thy call,
I come, to praise Thee with my heart and voice,
I come, with blood-bought sinners to rejoice;

I bless my dying day, I bless the grace
That gives me with Thy ransomed ones a place.
Now for eternity that grace to see,
Now for eternal songs to sing to Thee!!

"Lord, What Wouldst Thou Have Me to Do?"

Hast Thou, my Master, aught for me to do
    To honor Thee to-day?
Hast Thou a word of love to some poor soul,
    That I may say?

For see, this world that Thou hast made so fair,
    Within its heart is sad;
Thousands are lonely, thousands sigh and weep;
    But few are glad.

To which of them shall I stretch forth my hand,
    With sympathetic grasp?
Whose fainting form, for Thy dear sake, shall I
    Fondly enclasp?

They all are dear to Thee; and loving Thee,
    Dear are they all to me;
In every visage marred by grief and pain,
    Thy mark I see.

Straight from my heart, each day a blessing goes
    Warmly, through Thee, to theirs;
They are enfolded in my inmost soul,
    And in my prayers.

But which, among them all, is mine *to-day?*
    O guide my willing feet,
To some poor soul that fainting on the way
    Needs counsel sweet.

Or into some sick-room, where I may speak
    With tenderness of Thee;

And showing who and what Thou art, O Christ,
  Bid sorrow flee.

Or unto one whose straits call not for words;
  To one in want, in need;
Who will not counsel, but will take from me
  A loving deed.

Surely Thou hast some work for me to do!
  Oh, open Thou mine eyes,
To see how Thou wouldst choose to have it done,
  And where it lies!

Seeking the Water-Brooks

Hunted o'er valley, o'er plain and o'er mountain,
  Refuge none finding, relentless his foes;
Panteth the hart for the brook and the fountain,
  Panteth and thirsteth, nor seeks for repose.

Hunted, oh hunted this weary world over
  Refuge none finding my God, save in Thee,
Thus pants my soul Thine abode to discover,
  Thus stretches onward Thy glory to see.

Sorrow, temptation and sin fast pursuing,
  Seek for my soul, for its ruin and death,
Onward I fly, my weak forces renewing,
  Thirsting and fainting and panting for breath.

Dry is the land, is my soul's lamentation;
  Thirsting and panting, fast onward I flee,
Fleeing from sorrow and sin and temptation,
  Thirsting and panting, Oh God! after Thee!

The Prodigal

Into the Master's house my feet were led;
 An outcast's feet;
I drank the wine, tasted the living bread
 For angels meet.

Not as a servant did I waiting stand,
 For, wondrous grace!
Child of the house, I clasped the Master's hand,
 And saw his face.

Yet, with a child's caprice, I learned to dread
 That form divine;
Tasteless became the true, the living bread,
 Tasteless the wine.

Wild longings seized me with resistless might;
 I stole away
And in the wilderness passed night by night
 And day by day.

Oh, weary nights! Oh, days of sin and shame!
 Remorseful tears
Ooze from my heart, yearning to wash your name
 Off long past years!

Foot-sore, repentant, Master! unto Thee
 I crept once more—
More sinful, more forlorn, more foul to see,
 I gained Thy door.

Not as a child, but as a servant, Lord,
 I ventured nigh;
Trembling and waiting for a single word,
 Watching Thine eye;

Knowing I could give nothing for Thy grace,
 Do naught for Thee—

Still, still, I yearned to look upon Thy face,
    Look once—and flee!

And lingering thus, my Master heard my groans
    Drew gently nigh,
Pity and pardon in His gracious tones,
    Peace in His eye.

Trembling, into His house once more my feet
    Were safely led;
Once more re-placed upon my Master's seat
    I broke His bread.

Of bitter memories by Love beguiled,
    I sat His guest:
Dear Lord! of Thy repentant, trusting child
    Thou knowest the rest.

A Prayer for Love and Faith

I love Thee, my Savior! I love Thee! I love Thee!
Strong as a rock is my faith in Thy name;
Naught upon earth I desire above Thee;
My Joy and my Solace, my Hope and my Aim!

I love Thee! But oh, with a limited measure;
I trust Thee! But oh, I'm ashamed of my trust;
I call Thee my All, and I seek for a treasure
That lies mid life's turmoil, and gleams from its dust.

Oh, give me a love that the depths of my being
Shall stir into life that it never has known;
Love mighty in purpose, unselfish, far-seeing,
Grasping and proving to make me its own.

Give me a faith that shall ask Thee no question,
Shudder and shrink at no trial by fire;
Faith that is patient, that makes no suggestion,
Thou its sole Object, its single Desire!

Urge me to seek Thee! Impel me, allure me!
Penetrate down to the depths of my soul;
Thou whose vast pity alone can endure me,
Take me, oh take me—the whole, Lord, the whole.

Oh how I hate all my follies and seemings!
Loathe my self-love, my mistakes, and my sins;
Strength I have wasted in pitiful dreamings;
Nursing of fancies and petty chagrins!

Oh Thou All-Seeing, All-Loving, All-Knowing,
Penitent, weeping, I lie at Thy feet!
Take Thou this heart, with Thy love it is glowing,
Take this whole life that Thy faith has made sweet!

The Mystery of Life in Christ

I walk along the crowded streets, and mark
        The eager, anxious faces;
Wondering what this man seeks,
        what that heart craves,
        In earthly places.

Do I want any thing that they are wanting?
        Is each of them my brother?
Could we hold fellowship, speak heart to heart,
        Each to the other?

Nay, but I know not! only this I know,
        That sometimes merely crossing
Another's path, where life's tumultuous waves
        Are ever tossing,

He, as he passes, whispers in mine ear
        One magic sentence only,
And in the awful loneliness of crowds
        I am not lonely.

Ah, what a life is theirs who live in Christ;
    How vast the mystery!
Reaching in height to heaven, and in its depth
    The unfathomed sea!

Loving Christ for Himself Alone

I loved Thee once for what Thou wert to me,
God of my life and Savior of my soul;
    I loved to roll
The burden of my safety upon Thee.

I loved Thy gifts, and held them as Thy trust;
Looked at them often, clasped them to my heart,
    But would not part
At Thy behest, with one, save as I must.

I loved myself, and through myself I tried
To see Thy beauty, and behold Thy face;
    Yet had not grace,
To cast this medium dim in scorn aside.

I love Thee now, oh Christ! for what Thou art,
Love Thy perfections and Thy name adore,
    Recount them o'er,
And at Thy feet lay down a thankful heart.

And still I love Thy gifts, and know them all
To be kind tokens from my gracious Lord;
    But at a word
Will give them back to Thee at Thy recall.

And still I love myself,—alas, too well,
Yet do not see Thee through this glass defiled;
    Thy blessed child
Beholds Thy face, doth in Thy presence dwell.

Oh where are words to tell the joy unpriced
Of the rich heart, that breasting waves no more,
  Drifts thus to shore,
Laden with peace, and tending unto Christ!

"My Cup Runneth Over"

Jesus, I fain would sing a sweeter song
Than my glad heart has ever sung before;
For Thou, who hast been bountiful to me,
Hast filled my cup till it is running o'er.

Why hast Thou thus revealed Thyself to me?
Why hast Thy secret unto me made known?
Why singled me from many loving hearts,
Whispering these mysteries to me alone?

Thou art too good, too great, too wise, too kind;
And even while to see Thee I entreat,
My weakness puts Thee from me, and I cry
This is too great a joy, a bliss too sweet.

Oh stay Thine hand! I cannot, cannot bear
This weight of glory; cannot live, and see
The face that Thou in tender grace hast turned
On me, a sinful creature, even me.

Yes, I can bear Thy strokes, but not Thy love;
I can endure Thy frowns, but not Thy smile;
Frowns I deserve, and stripes I sorely need,
And Thine own choice has given them erewhile.

And yet amid my tears, my heart rings out
A richer song than songs it sang before;
For Thou who hast been bountiful to me,
Hast given a cup to-day that runneth o'er!

Hold Thou Me Up

"Hold Thou me up and I shall be safe."

I cannot trust myself, Jesus my Lord,
Hold Thou me up!
My feet had well nigh slipped, with Thine own word
Hold Thou me up!
Oh teach me how, and when, and where to go,
The path of safety I entreat to know.

I cannot walk alone; I am a child,
Hold Thou me up;
And yet to try my strength am oft beguiled;
Hold Thou me up!
Support me, lead me, keep me in Thy way
Be Thou my Surety, Thou my Strength and Stay.

Oh do not let me fall! I cling to Thee;
Hold Thou me up;
Be merciful in this great strait to me;
Hold Thou me up!
Let Thy strong hand prevent me; let Thy grace
Carry me safely past this slippery place.

For I have fallen, and I know its pain;
Hold Thou me up;
Fallen and risen, ris'n to fall again;
Hold Thou me up;
My weakness and my helplessness I know;
Hold Thou me up, I will not let Thee go!

The Safe Place

I went to Jesus with a prayer
Upon a suppliant's knee;
Low at His Cross I laid me down,
Nor asked His face to see,

Yet whispered in His ear the tale
　　No mortal ear could bear;
The story of a faithless heart;
　　And of its self-despair.

I told Him how my feet had slipped
　　How often gone astray;
How oft my heart refused to love,
　　My lips refused to pray.
In stammering words that none but He
　　Hearing could understand,
I made complaint of careless work
　　Done by a careless hand.

Of wasted hours, of idle words,
　　Of love oft waxing dim,
Of silence when a warmer heart
　　Had testified of Him.
I owned my weak and selfish ways;
　　How often all day long,
Moanings and sighs had filled His ears
　　To whom I owed a song.
And what said He? What whispered words
　　Responded unto mine?
Did He reproach me? Did His love
　　On me refuse to shine?

Nay, thus He spake, and bent Him low
　　To reach my anxious ear,
"My child, thou doest well to lie
　　As thou art lying here;
I *knew* thy human weakness, knew
　　Each lurking bosom-sin,
Knew it, and yet in loving grace
　　Thy heart I stooped to win.

"I knew that thou would'st often fall,
　　Poor work for Me would'st do,
Would'st give me only half thy love,
　　Give praises faint and few.

And yet I chose thee. Be content;
    And since thou canst not fly
To heights by dearer souls attained,
    Let it suffice to lie.

Here at My feet; it is a place
    To which My loved ones flee;
They find it sweet, and so shalt thou;
    'Tis a safe place for thee."

Yes, it *is* sweet, and it *is* safe!
    And here will I abide;
Sinful, and yet forgiven, sad,
    And yet so satisfied!

The New Song

"And they sang a new song."

There is a song I want to sing—
    Or want to learn to sing;
It is a song of praise to Thee,
    Jesus, my Lord and King.

Oh teach me all its varied notes,
    Its hidden melody,
Till I have learned to sing by heart,
    This song of praise to Thee.

I want to sing, while yet on earth,
    The tender, thankful strain
Of saints, who gladly near Thy throne,
    Make Thee their song's refrain.

For though I am not yet a saint,
    And though my praises ring
From an encumbered, earthly soul,
    I love the strains they sing.

And well I love, I know I love,
    Though truly not as they,
Thee, blessed Jesus whom I praise
    Feebly on earth to-day;

While there's a song I want to sing—
    Or want to learn to sing;
A blessed song of love to Thee,
    Jesus, my Lord and King.

Confession

Jesus, is there a spot where I can hide
    To be alone with Thee,
Where I can whisper in Thy listening ear
    My earnest plea?

Oh I do long so to be sanctified;
    To be emancipate
From fellowship with evil, and to feel
    Of sin no weight.

Surely I love Thee;—and yet, if I do—
    Whence comes this earthly taint?
Surely I love to pray,—but loving it,
    Whence this restraint?

Is there a soul on earth so clogged as mine?
    That mounts on such poor wing?
Surely there is no song of praise so mean
    As that I sing.

Yet it is eager for exultant flight
    And sometimes how it longs
To pour into Thy loving, gracious ear,
    Exultant songs!

Oh blest are they whose conflicts are no more,
    Whose love flows forth to Thee

A restless tide that ebbs and flows
Like a deep sea!

The Power of Christ's Blood

Oh is it possible that I, a sinner,
          Shall be, one day, a saint?
That life's hard conflict ever shall be over,
          And ended all complaint?

Shall I be cleansed and washed, and then invited
          To be the Master's guest?
Has He a bridal robe for me provided,
          In which I shall be drest?

It cannot be! It seems as if such records
          As stand against my name,
Could not be wiped away, must stand forever
          To be my lasting shame.

Oh Jesus, make me know what half I'm knowing
          The power of Thy blood,
Plunge Thou this faithless and this sinful creature
          Deep, deep within its flood!

Love to Christ

Dear Savior, if I love Thee not
     I know not what love means;
I live upon Thy smile, I warm,
     I sun me in its beams;
And drinking at Thy fountain sweet
     Care not for other streams.

But do I give a generous love?
     Is it so rich and free,
That I can give no more, dear Lord,

No more be asked of me?
Is my heart really filled as full
　　As human heart can be?

Nay, if it be, yet fill it, Lord,
　　With more than it can hold;
Give me that I may give, until
　　My loving arms enfold,
Not Thee alone, but Thy whole world
　　In myriads untold!

The Broken Wing

Have patience and have faith
　　The surgeon saith,
Suffer awhile this irksomeness of pain;
This broken limb shall soon be well again;
　　Yea, what is more,
Be stronger for all service than before.

　　So come I, broken heart,
　　To ease thy smart,
With promises the future shall make good.
Bear thou in patience Sorrow's solitude,
　　For she, at length
Will lead thee forth in manliness and strength.

　　Yes, and in strength unknown
　　When joy alone
Held thee within her nerveless arms, until
Thou hadst lost courage, lost all force of will.
　　God will restore
That which He brake,
　　and give it strength the more.

　　Will make thee strong and wise
　　To sympathize;
For thou wilt know to soothe,
　　with tender hand,

The sufferings thou hast learned to understand;
        And to the weak
What words of inspiration thou wilt speak!

        Thou wilt be strong in love;
        Soft as a dove,
Yet hovering as on eagle's wings around
The spot where loneliness and grief are found,
        And healing bring,
In grateful memory of a broken wing.

        Thou wilt have strength unpriced
        To work for Christ!
To testify of Him whom pain alone
Could to the human soul Himself make known;
        To watch and pray,
Stronger upon each morrow than to-day.

God Is For Me

"When I cry unto Thee then shall mine enemies turn back:
This I know: for God is for me." —Psalm 56:9

        Turn back, mine enemy, unmoved
            Thy wiles, thy snares I see;
        Turn back, for when I cry to God
            I know He is for me.

        Thy day is over; I no more
            Thy willing slave can be,
        For I have learned to cry to God;
            I know He is for me.

        Hence with thy strong delusions, hence,
            I parley not with thee,
        But mid thy temptings cry to God,
            I know He is for me.

        Ah, if thou knewest as I know
            The God to whom I flee,

Thou wouldst not think to gain mine ear;
I know He is for me!

Festal Days

Thou hast thy festal days, my soul,
    Thou hast had one to-day!
How gracious was the Master's voice,
    How sweet it was to pray.
In all the world oh can there be,
    A greater joy than thine,
Who hast seen Jesus, and hast felt
    His love upon thee shine?

Yet crave not, ask not, that thy life
    Be fashioned of such days;
Take what God gives, and question not
    The mystery of His ways;
Sit at His table when His voice
    Shall to that table call;
Yet when He bids not, be content
    With crumbs that from it fall.

Oh blessed Jesus! Thou art good
    When I may see Thy face,
And just as good, when though I cry
    Thou wilt not grant that grace.
Giving, I love Thee in Thy gifts,
    Thy gracious Name adore.
Withholding, I will love Thee, Lord
    And cling to Thee the more!

Speak of Christ

Oh speak to me of Christ! No name
    Falls on my ravished ear

With half the music, half the charm,
    That makes it bliss to hear
A loving voice pronounce that word
    As one who holds it dear.

Hast thou not in some favored hour
    Beheld Him face to face,
And canst thou not make known to me
    Its beauty and its grace,
And lure me on to seek for Him
    In some familiar place?

Hast Thou not feasted on His word,
    And found it meat indeed,
And canst thou not a fragment spare
    On which my soul may feed,
Some promise, whispered by His lips
    To meet my sorest need?

Has He not revelations made
    In sacred hours to thee,
That thou canst hold as sacred trust,
    And yet confide to me
Who love, but fain would love Him more,
    Have seen, yet more would see?

Yes, speak of Christ! As one who speaks
    Of his familiar friend,
As one who sees Him every day,
    May on His steps attend,
As one who oft, on reverent knee
    Before Him loves to bend.

Speak with a living warmth, a glow
    That shall my heart enflame,
And with thy rich and conscious love
    Put my poor love to shame,
Until I, too, have learned to speak
    That dearest, dearest Name!

Not Fit to Go

I have been forth upon my Master's work
    And yet I know
I was not fit His work to undertake,
    Not fit to go.

I fancied that He sent me, that He said
    "The work is Mine,
But lo I have entrusted it to thee,
    And it is thine."

Alas, I went with banner floating high,
    Strong in my pride;
And bitterly came back, with my whole self
    Dissatisfied.

Dear Lord, art Thou so poor?
    Couldst Thou not find?
    A hand more meet
To bear Thy gifts? See, it is stained and soiled,
    And my tired feet

Are all adust with wanderings from Thee;
    I blush with shame,
When I go laden with the Bread of Life,
    Or speak Thy name.

Oh cleanse these hands,
    and from these feet shake off
    The dust of sin;
Rid me of all curses, make me pure
    Without, within.

For blessed are the hands that wait on Thee,
    And blest the feet
That speed them on their mission
    And that know
        Thy service sweet.

With Great Delight

"I sat down under His shadow with great delight."
"I will abide under the shadow of the Almighty."

With great delight!
Yes, so I sat and rested in His shade,
When of the burden of the day,
and of its glare afraid;
I felt myself protected, saved, looked up and saw His face,
How beautiful in tenderness,
how wonderful in grace!

With great delight!
Life pressed me sore, I knew not where to flee,
In all the world I saw no room,
no sphere, no work for me;
He called me to this sheltered spot, rebuking my despair,
I went, and oh the joy I found,
the peace I tasted there!

With great delight!
A loving friend had fallen at my side,
My eyes were blinded by my tears,
my heart within me died;
I staggered from the empty world into this dear retreat,
And found my bitter grief assuaged,
yea found my sorrow sweet.

With great delight!
My heart is fixed, its endless wants I know,
Forth from this shelter I henceforth
will never, never go;
Here in the shadow of God's love, forever I'll abide,
So glad, so blest, so sure, so safe;
so more than satisfied!

Oh Come to Christ

Oh come to Christ! a single glance
  Would melt your doubts away,
One glance would flood you with His light
  And an eternal day.

Oh come to Christ! He waits for you,
  Long has He waiting stood,
Stooping to ask you for your heart,
  Yearning to do you good.

Oh come to Christ! the world has proved
  To thee a broken reed;
Thou canst not trust what always fails
  In time of sorest need.

Oh come to Christ! for peace, for rest,
  For all thy heart can crave,
For triumph over pain and loss,
  The deathbed and the grave.

They Have Been With Jesus

"And they took knowledge of them, that they had been with Jesus."

Have they not been with Jesus?
  See how their faces shine,
With a radiance unearthly,
  with a glow almost divine,
His mark is on their foreheads,
  His grace is in their smile,
Every feature is the witness
  of a spirit without guile.

They must have been with Jesus!
  for truly they alone,
Who dwell with Him can ever
  catch the sweetness of His tone,

What tenderness, what earnestness,
   is breathed in every note,
What thrills of joy melodious
   within its cadence float.

They have been much with Jesus!
   no better proof it needs
Than the beauty and the kindliness
   of all their holy deeds,
Theirs are the hands that minister
   to want and to distress,
That into every bitter cup
   a healing cordial press.

They have been long with Jesus!
   within His blessed school,
They have yielded meek obedience
   to lesson and to rule,
The wisdom of their teachings
   mark the graces of their speech,
Which guides the weak and ignorant,
   yet may the highest reach.

Yes, they have been with Jesus!
   and counting all things dross,
Have bent, for His dear sake,
   beneath the burden of His cross;
What chastened, humbled souls are theirs,
   how unto His akin,
Thrice bless-ed are ye gracious ones,
   all heaven is yours to win.

The Friend of the Lonely

With Christ ever present, I should not be lonely
   Alone in mid ocean, or desert afar;
I long for Thy presence! I watch for Thy coming
   Who art Sun of my day, who of night art my Star!

I have known Thee in sorrow, in joy I have known Thee,
  Thou hast wiped away tears, in my gladness been glad;
Thou hast pitied me, cared for me, borne with my follies,
  Been with me when happy, been with me when sad.

Where art Thou now? of the lonely I'm lonely—
  Mid plenty I'm starving, with nothing sufficed
Friends gather round me, I know them, I love them,
  But oh I am weary, aweary for Christ.

Ah, let me be weary! But let me be patient;
  If Thou hast been mine, Lord, then still Thou art mine;
Weeping through midnight may last, but the morning,
  Sooner or late through the darkness shall shine.

Under the Rod

In vain I seek to hide it from myself,
  My heart is sorrowful, is full of tears;
New grief awakes the echoes of the past,
  I live again through pangs of parted years.

Dear Jesus, it is well! here at Thy feet
  I thank Thee for the past, the present press
Close to my heart of hearts; I love Thy blows,
  Would not evade them, would not wish them less.

How wise, how good Thou art! my wayward will
  Left to itself would lead me all astray,
My wisdom is all ignorance, nor can
  My blinded eyes trace out Thy perfect way.

I want to be like Thee, I want to dwell
  Forever with Thee, and full well I know
Thy path is lowly, full of thorns, yet there
  Where Thou hast been Thy followers must go.

I want a spirit that shall strive and cry
  No more, dear Lord, but meek and humble be,

I want the lowly temper of a child,
   Its weanedness, and its docility.

Thou who hast sent this sorrow, send with it
   A supple will that yields itself to Thine;
That blends itself, is lost in Thy dear will,
   That henceforth shall of naught say,
      "This is mine!"

Yea, on the pathway of this sorest pain,
   I come to meet Thee, wilt Thou condescend,
To let me find Thee in it, who art more,
   Ten thousand more than dearest earthly friend.

The Work of Peace

Let me not wait for a new grief to prove me,
     But now while all around me wears a smile,
Dear Jesus, with new love oh let me love Thee,
     With gladder thoughts of Thee the way beguile.

I want to love Thee more, to feel Thee dearer,
     To honor Thee in word and look and tone,
I want to feel Thee ever drawing nearer,
     To be more Thine, and to be less mine own.

Sorrow in times now past has often laid me
     Humble, and empty, down at Thy dear feet,
She only broken-hearted could have made me,
     And taught me to find tribulation sweet.

Shall peace and joy do less for me than sorrow?
     Canst Thou not make them also lay me low?
From them too also may my soul not borrow
     Guidance to Thee? of Thee yet more to know?

Oh lead me on, my Savior, bide no halting—
     On to the secret spot where Thou dost dwell—

Lead me beyond temptation's rude assaulting—
Led on by joy or sorrow, all is well!

Why Empty and Sad?

Other hearts are full, are full of Jesus,
    Why is thine so empty and so sad?
Is it not His work to cheer and please us,
    Is there nothing in Him to make glad?

Say not thou are stript of all thy treasures—
    Rather say the bands that held me fast,
Have been rent in twain that higher pleasures
    My poor, starving soul may seek at last.

Ah, no words there are to tell the sweetness
    Of the soul, that, letting all things go,
Finds itself at rest in Christ's completeness,
    Finds Him solace for its every woe.

Yet the song has rung through all the ages,
    Oft the story sufferers have told;
How He lighted up life's darkest pages,
    Bound, with his own hands, the tale in gold!

Come and try, thou sad and sorrowing spirit,
    What He is in loss, and grief, and pain;
Thou for mourning shall His peace inherit,
    And for sighs take up a joyful strain.

Rest in Thee

"Our hearts are restless, till they find their rest in Thee."—Augustine

Ah, there is much in this strange life that saddens,
    And much that brings discomfort and unrest,
And there is much that beautifies and gladdens,
    Foretaste of heaven's fulness mid the blest.

Sadness looks downward; sees the shadows lengthen,
    Mid graves of the departed loves to roam;
Gladness looks upward, ebbing faith to strengthen,
    Lives in the promised land and bears right home.

I know them both. I have clasped hands with sorrow,
    And through the ranks of long succeeding years,
Have said I cannot boast me of to-morrow,
    My bread a stony grief, my drink but tears.

And I know joy; the joy that is victorious
    O'er pain and smart, that triumphs in despair,
That looks at suffering and declares it glorious
    To weep with Christ, His fellowship to share.

And now if He should come and freely offer
    To let me make of one of these my choice,
Should I, with grateful heart, accept the proffer,
    And in this freedom of my will rejoice?

Oh no! I want not freedom! Give me rather
    Sense of Thy will, my God, opposed to mine,
I am a little child, and Thou my Father,
    I have no rights, they all are merged in Thine.

Give me or pain or gladness at Thy pleasure,
    Give what Thy wisdom and Thy love may choose,
But be Thou of my soul the hidden treasure,
    And all that soul's defilement let me lose.

For oh, I would be Thine, would walk beside Thee,
    Would know Thee who Thou art, Thy face would see,
My heart is fixed, whatever may betide me,
    It shall have rest, for there is rest in Thee.

Christ on the Shore

Lord, blessed be Thy name that Thou dost stand
　　Upon life's shore to regulate the flow
Of its wide ocean; that Thy grace has planned
　　Its boundaries, doth all its motions know.

For if its tides were ever coming in,
　　All would give way before its tumult wild;
We should become the sport of pain and sin,
　　Tossed on the raging billows, like a child.

Cheer then, thou tempted soul! though for awhile
　　The tempest sweep thee with resistless might,
The tide shall ebb, and thou again shalt smile
　　On peaceful waters, sparkling through the night.

And cheer thyself, poor heart! this storm of pain
　　That sweeps thee all before it, shall be stayed,
The Son of God will hurl it back again,
　　Whose mighty hand hath earth's foundations laid.

Thus far the waves may come, but when they reach
　　His chosen limits, thou art safe, art free;
He lets them loose upon thee, but to teach
　　How strong, how merciful, His arm can be.

Thou art no thing of chance; His watchful eye
　　Notes just how far thou on the shore art thrown;
Bruised, buffeted, bewildered, thou mayst be,
　　But dost not suffer friendless and alone.

Cheer thee, faint heart! Beyond the ebb and flow
　　Of mortal shores, there shines a crystal sea,
Where thou shalt lie at rest, and cease to know
　　Floods of temptation, waves of agony.

There ever dwells on that eternal shore,
　　The risen Son of God; to make it thine,

The fearful winds and waves of time He bore,
    Tempted, yet sinless; suffering, yet divine.

Cheer thee, sad heart! In smiling ranks there stand
    Millions of rescued souls, for aye at rest;
Rough winds and billows tossed them to the strand,
    Not rougher are the waves that thou must breast.

At Christ's Table

I got to meet Thee at Thy table, Lord,
        Hear Thou my prayer,
The inmost, deepest longing of my heart,
        And meet me there.

The wedding-garment of Thy righteousness
        Do Thou prepare,
And with the hands that once for me were pierced,
        Enrobe me there.

Reveal to me the burden of the cross
        Thou once didst bear,
Let me too bend beneath it and behold
        And love Thee there.

And when the feast is spread, choose Thou a great
        Or scanty share
For me, as best it pleaseth Thee, and deign
        To feed me there.

Sweet festival! Sweet Lord! Sweet bread and wine
        I will repair
To it in love and silent gratitude;
        O Christ, be there!

Is the Heart Ready?

Lord, is my heart prepared to meet
 The answer to its prayers,
To stoop at Thy behest, beneath
 The cross that Jesus bears,
To smart beneath the scorn and shame
That they must taste who own His name?

Thou who canst penetrate the folds
 That hide my feeble faith,
Bring forth and try it, heeding not
 What my poor nature saith—
I would be fully known to Thee,
As I would have Thee known to me.

Ah, let my words fall far below
 The fervor of my soul,
Let me not offer Thee a part
 But freely give the whole,
Jesus my Lord, in asking this,
I ask both poverty and bliss.

For he who empty is alone,
 Can by Thy grace be filled,
The thirsty, hungry soul, Thy hand
 Alone to reach is skilled;
And yet how faint that soul must be
Ere it will own its all to Thee!

But when, with hardly strength to cry,
 It casts its languid eye
Upon Thy riches, a new life
 Will through its pulses fly;
Thenceforth how truly it will rest,
An infant on its mother's breast.

"God is Here"

Within a desert's rough embrace
    A single flower was thrown;
Denied communion with her race
She stood in this wide dwelling-place,
    Neglected and alone.

Yet, mid this changeless solitude
    She sighed not to be great,
Secure from pride's impatient mood,
It was her pleasant daily food,
    Her Master's time to wait.

A weary traveler passed that way–
    That weary way, at length,–
With trustless heart and faint, he lay
Upon the sands, to weep away
    His manliness and strength.

The little stranger flower was nigh–
    Her voice was on his ear,
And faith and joyful trust, sprang high
To weary limb and heart and eye,
    From her brief, *"God is here!"*

Uprose the fainting man, and blessed
    The truth, and blessed the flower;
Companionship and life and rest,
As future paths his footsteps pressed,
    Were his, from that bright hour.

Oh thou! who livest a useless thing,
Thine errand here much questioning,
    "Hope on! Hope ever!"
Dwelling from worldly toil apart,
Thy voice through some distrusting heart
    Shall thrill forever.
Wait on, wait on, do not thou fear,
If thou canst only whisper, *"God is here!"*

The School

The closing two lines are to be found upon Mrs. Prentiss' tombstone

We are scholars, nothing but scholars,
Little children at school,
Learning our daily lessons,
Subject to law and rule.

Life is the school, and the Master
Is the Man Jesus Christ,
We are His charity scholars,
His the teaching unpriced.

Slowly we learn, all His patience
Is hourly put to the test;
But often the slowest and dullest,
He pities and loves the best.

Still, we sit at the feet of our Master,
Very low at His feet.
Study the lessons He sets us,
Sometimes lessons repeat.

Some of the lessons are pleasant,
Pleasant, and easy to learn;
The page of our task-book simple,
Simple and easy to turn.

But anon the reading is painful,
Studied mid sighing and tears;
We stammer and falter over it,
Do not learn it for years.

Yet that is no fault of the Master;
All His lessons are good;
Only our childish folly
Leaves them misunderstood.

And still we go on, learning,
    And learning to love our school;
Learning to love our Master,
    Learning to love His rule.

And by and by, we children
    Shall grow into perfect men,
And the loving, patient Master
    From school will dismiss us then.

No more tedious lessons,
    No more sighing and tears,
But a bound into home immortal,
    And blessed, blessed years!

My Kindred

Oh that this heart, with grief so well acquainted
Might be a fountain rich and sweet and full
For all the weary that have fall'n and fainted
In life's parched desert, thirsty, sorrowful!

Come unto me, my kindred! I enfold you
In an embrace to sufferers only known,
Close to this heart I tenderly will hold you,
Suppress no sigh, keep back no tear, no groan.

Yes, weep upon this bosom, that upheaving
With anguish upon anguish, knows full well,
Of grief that had not respite or reprieving,
Of tides that on a shoreless ocean swell.

And can I give you joy and rest and healing?
Can I, a human sufferer at best,
Restore the current calm of peaceful feeling,
And to your weariness give welcome rest?

Nay, but I know who can! My Lord and Master
Give me brave words with which to speak of Thee,

Oh let my grateful tears flow sweeter, faster,
At the remembrance of Thy sympathy!

Thou Man of Sorrows, teach my lips, that often
Have told the sacred story of my woe,
To speak of Thee till stony griefs I soften,
Till hearts that know Thee not, learn Thee to know.

Till peace takes place of storm and agitation,
Till lying on the current of Thy will,
There shall be glorying in tribulation,
And Christ Himself each empty heart shall fill.

Oh Jesus! Sweet Chastiser! Thanks I render
For aching heart, for pain-contracted brow,
For thus alone I learned how true, how tender,
How beautiful, how beautiful art Thou!

Christ Asks for All

A jealous lover art Thou, oh my God,
  Asking my all from me;
Is it too much to give? Can I refuse
  This all to Thee?

I cannot trust myself, for while I say,
  All that I have is Thine,
. There may be hidden in my inmost heart
  Some thing yet mine.

I may be clinging, though I know it not,
  To some long-cherished joy;
I may be clasping, with a childish heart,
  Some childish toy.

I would not have it thus! I would let go
  Of every outward thing,
That I with empty hands, my dearest Lord,
  To Thee may cling.

Thou art enough to satisfy my heart;
>   Long years have taught me this,
Take all, but leave Thyself, I cannot ask
>   A greater bliss.

The Unseen Spirit

When busy with my household tasks
>   throughout the live-long day
An unseen Spirit walks with me
>   and over me holds sway.

When I walk the city's crowded streets,
>   that Spirit walks with me
Interpreting and putting home
>   each object that I see.

When through the woods I wander
>   lost in wonder and delight
That Spirit still is with me
>   making every thing look bright.

When friends are clustered round me,
>   the Spirit too, is there,
Making loving hearts more loving,
>   and fair faces seem more fair.

He speaks to me in whispers
>   that I alone can hear,
Speaks of God and Christ and heaven,
>   in accents sweet and clear.

He urges me to faithfulness,
>   He quickens me in prayer,
He utters precious promises
>   in moments of despair.

Do I love this unseen Spirit,
   do I follow His behest,
Do I pray Him to abide with me
   forever in my breast?

Ah yes! I truly love Him!
   but for Him my truant heart
From every holy habit
   forever would depart.

But for Him I should relapse
   into worldliness and sin,
Should prove a traitor shameful,
   and let the Tempter in.

Oh blessed, Holy Spirit!
   Oh never, never leave
My heart a single moment,
   lest I Thy love should grieve.

With Thee I can do all things,
   but if Thou turn away,
I, faithless and ungrateful,
   should forever go astray!

A Prayer for Charity

O Lord, Thou pitiest more than Thou dost blame
   My sin and shame:—
When I, a fallen creature, do condemn
My brother-man, and do his sin contemn,
Thou to the downcast sinner bring'st release,
"Neither do I condemn thee, go in peace."

Oh for a spirit unto Thine akin!
   Oh but to win
A heart of love, a patience like to Thine,
To gain a charity, a love, divine!

In this sad moment when I see my need,
Grant Thou the blessing rare for which I plead.

And when my brother falls, help me to cry
        This might be I;
Thus I, too, should descend without God's grace!
Grant me to look into his downcast face,
With sweet compassion shining upon mine
In heartfelt memory of deeds of Thine!

At Jesus' Feet

There is a spot where tempted souls
      May find a dear retreat:
They fly from sin and self, and lie
      At Jesus' feet.

In vain upon their heads, the storms
      Of life may rudely beat,
Grief cannot harm the soul that lies
      At Jesus' feet.

My soul, upon life's dizzy heights
      Beware to take thy seat,
Leave not the valley, but abide
      At Jesus' feet.

Would'st thou in peace, and joy and love
      And gladness, stand complete?
Seek it in penitence and faith,
      At Jesus' feet.

A Steadfast Heart

Keep my heart steadfast, dearest Lord
      For earth's allurements shine,
And bid me turn mine eye away
      From looking into Thine.

Oh keep me steadfast! Earthly tones
    Fall sweetly on my ear,
And while I pause to list to them
    Thy voice I cannot hear.

Oh keep me steadfast! Human smiles
    Delude my childish heart;
While rapt in them how easily
    From Thee I can depart.

Yes, keep me, keep me, for myself
    I cannot, cannot keep;
Keep me by day, keep me by night
    O Thou who dost not sleep.

Death, a Friend and Brother

I think of Death as of a friend and brother
    Who, some bright day, will come and call for me
And lead me to the presence of Another
    With whom I long have pined at home to be.

I know not in what form, or mid what guises
    He will approach me, only this I know,
If he at midnight or at noon surprises,
    I shall clasp hands with him and gladly go.

Have I then nothing that to earth can bind me?
    Has all my oil of gladness been consumed?
Shall not I cast one lingering look behind me,
    Regretting flowers that but for me have bloomed?

Ah, there are few on earth whose human treasures
    More manifold, and costlier are, than mine;
My life is full of joys and full of pleasures,
    Full of the oil of gladness and its wine.

But oh, to go to be with Christ forever!
　To see His face, His wondrous voice to hear!
Never again from Him I love to sever,
　Never to miss His accents on my ear!

So then, my brother, Death, for thee I'm ready;
　I wait, yet woo thee not, abide God's time;
My heart is fixed, my footsteps calm and steady;
　So lead me on to destiny sublime.

Lead me to Christ, lead from all power of sinning,
　Lead me to those who in His image shine;
This will of life be only the beginning,
　And birth, not death, through thee,
　　　　shall then be mine.

God's Saints

God has His saints upon the earth
　　Who love Him more than I,
Whose hearts are more attuned to His,
　　And yet I know not why.

Who has more reason to fall down
　　Before the Father's face,
To thank Him for His sparing love,
　　For His redeeming grace?

Whose tears of gratitude should gush
　　From fountains full and free,
At memory of more tenderness
　　Than Thou hast shown to me?

Lord, make me love Thee! Take my heart,
　　Establish there Thy throne,
I would be Thine, would have Thee mine,
　　O make me all Thine own.

My Expectation is from Thee

Lord, I have nothing, in myself am naught,
    Weak as a bruised reed Thou findest me;
And yet I dare to call myself Thy child,
    Because my expectation is from Thee.

I am so poor in grace, so weak in faith,
    Seek Thee so feebly on the bended knee;
And yet I must keep seeking, still aspire
    Because my expectation is from Thee.

I long so for Thy presence, yet how oft
    My sins constrain me from Thy face to flee;
I grieve, I falter, but hold on my way
    Because my expectation is from Thee.

I do the deeds I would not do, leave undone
    The gracious work that should completed be;
I am ashamed and sorry, yet hope on,
    Because my expectation is from Thee.

And the dread enemy of my poor soul
    Tempts me to yield and fail; but even he
Gives place at mention of Thy dearest name
    Because my expectation is from Thee.

So self-renouncing, desperate in myself,
    My fallen ruins I can calmly see,
For when I poorest am, all lost and gone,
    My only expectation is from Thee.

What Christ Can Be

Oh that some faithful soul could tell
    What Jesus Christ can be,
To the distracted soul that sinks
    In sorrow's briny sea,

And casts a last despairing look
    To His wide sympathy.

No mother's hand with clasp so soft,
    So true, so kind can press,
And of the gentle, loving tone
    A mother's voice has less;
Yea, she that bare thee is but rough
    To Jesus' tenderness.

Come and behold what Jesus is;
    Into His gracious ear
Pour all the story of thy grief,
    Whisper thine every fear,
And on His sympathizing breast,
    Weep out thine every tear.

Then first the risen Son of God
    Shall unto thee be known,
Then only canst thou feel his heart
    Respond to every groan,
And echo to the bursting sigh,
    The plaintive, helpless moan.

Ah joyful hearts that know not grief
    Can never Jesus know;
He must be learned in darksome nights,
    Where bitter fountains flow,
Where souls are floated off to sea
    By tides of earthly woe.

There have I met Thee, dearest Lord!
    And oh how passing sweet,
Was to my sinking soul, the sound
    Of Thine approaching feet–
To point Thee out to drowning ones,
    Oh make me, make me meet!

The Sea of Fire

Ah, dearest Master, art Thou really purging
    My sinful soul within this sea of fire?
To deeper consecration art Thou urging,
    Plunging me lower but to call me higher?

Small is the pain, not wearisome the bearing
    The cross Thy hand in mercy lays on me;
Oh let it urge me from the path ensnaring,
    And lead me nearer, ever nearer Thee.

Pain, in itself, I love not, but its teachings
    Have been so precious, so have made Thee known,
That my whole soul is making tender reachings,
    To meet it as it comes, to hear its tone.

Oh come Thou with it! I am very weary
    Of prosperous days that hide Thy blessed face;
The brightest sunshine makes the landscape dreary,
    That is not luminous with Thine own grace.

Staying There–Coming Back

We laid her tenderly away,
within her silent bed–
A bed of living flowers of love,
 trees waving overhead;

With prayers and tears and parting hymn,
we left our darling there,
And we came back to life's old work,
to miss her everywhere.

We had a single path before,
and walked it hand in hand,
But she was weary, stopped to rest,
was parted from our band;

We left her lying there alone,
a smile upon her face,
And we came back, as tired as she,
to see her vacant place;

Left her to sleep in dreamless peace,
beneath those guardian trees,
Came back to nights of wakeful grief,
and speechless agonies,

Came back to grapple with our hearts,
to falter on our way,
To find no language for our grief,
no words with which to pray.

Left her in garments that the dust
of sin can never soil,
Hers all the joy and all the rest,
and ours all the toil.

Farewell, beloved! all is well,
we gladly leave thee there,
Come not thou back again to us
to join us in life's care;

Our turn will come in God's own time,
and we shall sleep with thee,
Where birds can sing, and flowerets bloom,
and grass wave peacefully–

Till then thy flesh shall rest in hope,
and we will wait the day
When tender hands shall lay us down,
to sleep our grief away.

Draw Nearer !

Draw nearer, O my Savior, to my soul,
    For Thou art all, and all in all, to me,
Because I feel Thee near I want Thee more,
    Because I love Thee would more loving be.

I am so glad in Thee! A single smile
    A single glance from Thee, can rapture wake,
That finds no words with which to tell its tale,
    And with its joy my heart is like to break.

Draw nearer, nearer yet, reveal Thyself
    To me, Thy child, and oh dear Lord, do Thou,
If Thou hast any blessings in reserve,
    Open Thine hand and give those blessings now.

Thou canst give nothing that I do not need,
    For I am very poor, and if I might
Choose for myself, I would not dare to choose,
    I am too ignorant to ask aright.

And when I pray Thee to crowd out of me
    This monster, Self, and then to enter in
And take possession, as a peaceful Guest,
    Do I not ask deliverance from sin?

Do I not ask, within the compass small
    Of these few words, all that there is to give?
Come then, my Savior, make Thyself a home
    Within this breast, and ever in it live.

Self gone forever, do Thou reign, O Christ,
    The Conq'rer of the conquered, and for aye,
Over each spring of action and of thought,
    Hold Thou within me undisputed sway!

"And Ye are Christ's"

"Ye are not your own, bought," etc.
"If the Son therefore shall make you free, ye shall be free indeed."

And we are Christ's! What precious words,
    And oh! the wondrous thought,
That we are not our own but His,
    That He our souls has bought.

Poor slaves to sin and self, how hard
    How wearisome our lot,
We ate the bread of servitude,
    Toiled ever, rested not.

But Christ is Master now, and He
    Has set the captive free,
We weep no more, but sing the song,
    Of perfect liberty.

Yes, we are free to live for Him,
    Free to accept His grace,
To sing His praises, love His name,
    To see His dearest face.

Such is the freedom that our hearts
    Have fondly learned to crave,
The freedom that the Master's hand
    In loving bounty gave.

Yes, we are Christ's, His freedmen we,
    We are both bond and free,
Free by His choice and bond by ours–
    So let us ever be.

Wherein to Glory

"Let him that glorieth glory in this, that he understandeth and knoweth me."
Jeremiah 9:24

Lord, have I anything of which to boast,
    Of aught to glory,
Who of myself can only sigh, and tell
    The old, sad story?

Ah yes! for Thou hast stooped low down to me,
    Hast kindly sought me,
And who and what Thou art through long long years
    Hast taught and taught me.

Slowly I learned, for I was dull of brain,
    Cold in affection;
I was a heedless scholar, giddy, childish,
    Without reflection.

Yet now, my Teacher patient, Thee I know,
    Glory in knowing!
Each hour, each day, a grace, a beauty new,
    To me is showing.

Absorbed in this lesson, all about me
    Looks dim and meager,
To learn it wholly, learn it all by heart,
    How am I eager!

Oh condescend to tell me, then my Master
    The whole dear story,
And Thy rapt listener with grateful joy
    In Thee shall glory!

"Is It Well With the Child?"

Yes, it is well! For he has gone from me,
From my poor care, my human fallacy,
Straight to the Master's school, the Shepherd's love.
Blessed are they whose training is above!
He will grow up in Heaven, will never know
The conflicts that attend our life below.
He from his earliest consciousness, shall walk
With Christ Himself in glory; he shall talk
With sinless little children, and his ear
No sound discordant, no harsh word shall hear.
Nay, but I have no words with which to tell,
How well it is with him—how well, how well!

"Is It Well With Thee?"

Yes, it is well! For while with "anguish wild,"
I gave to God who asked him, my child,
He gave to me strong faith, and peace and joy;
Gave me these blessings when he took my boy.
He gave Himself to me; in boundless grace
Within my deepest depths He took His place;
Made heaven look home-like, made my bleeding heart
In all the grief of other hearts take part;
Brought down my pride, burnt up my hidden dross,
Made me fling down the world and clasp the cross
Ah how my inmost soul doth in me swell,
When I declare that all with me is well!

Go and Tell Jesus

Oh aching heart, oh restless brain,
    Go and tell Jesus of thy pain;
He knows thee, loves thee, and His eye
    Beams with divinest sympathy.

Go and tell Jesus; human ear
       Thy mournful story may not hear;
Keep nothing back, for thee He cares,
       His patient heart thy burden bears.

Go and tell Jesus; well He knows
       The human heart; its pangs, its throes;
He will not fail Thee, He will be
       Friend, Comforter, and Peace to thee.

Go and tell Jesus; never yet,
       Did He a breaking heart forget;
Press closely to His bleeding side,
       There, there thou shalt be satisfied.

A Wish

Oh that with ready grace my heart could give
       What God requires;
That there within it lived no grasping will
       No fond desires.

It grieves, it pains me that I do not fly
       O Christ, to Thee,
To lay this treasure at Thy feet, with sweet
       Alacrity.

Yet take it from me; if I love it much,
       I love Thee more,–
But pity, as Thou takest, for it leaves
       My heart so sore!

Healing

Low in the dust of self-abasement lying,
O'er a poor, wasted life my heart is sighing,
       Lord Jesus, heal my soul!

I have sought riches, glory, comfort, pleasure;
In Thee I saw no beauty, sought no treasure;
    Lord Jesus, heal my soul!

On husks the swine do eat I have been feeding,
I have resisted all Thy tender pleading;
    Lord Jesus, heal my soul!

How sorrowful, how spent I am, how weary,
Oh in this desert place so dark and dreary,
    Lord Jesus, heal my soul!

Weariness

Ah is there, anywhere, a sorer heart,
        Than this sore heart of mine?
Jesus, have mercy on me, let me lay
        Its griefs on Thine.

If Thou dost fail me, everything will fail;
        Pain be too hard to bear;
Then dost Thou pity me that I am sad?
        Lord, dost Thou care?

All eyes, save mine, may weep, but not for me
        Is the refreshing tear;
My tears are prayers, are speechless sighs and groans;
        O, dost Thou hear?

The Orange-Tree

Be like the faithful plant that not content
    With bearing fruitage as a yearly store,
While that fruit ripens, blossoms out anew,
That they who plucked may come and pluck once more.

Let those who seek thee find that blossoms rare
　　Deck thy meek bosom as with bridal grace,
Sweet charity adorn thee, tender smiles
　　Light up and render beautiful thy face.

And then surprise them with a harvest full
　　Of glorious deeds, who fancied they should find
Fragrance and loveliness, but did not dream
　　To gather also food for heart and mind.

Ever at Work

Ever at work, my weary hands
　　Might never folded be;
New tasks were ever given, and
　　There was no rest for me.

Others sat quietly at ease
　　From toilsome labor free;
I ceased not, for the Master said
　　There was no rest for me.

The busy world lay down at night
　　And slept right peacefully;
I could not sleep, upon my bed
　　There was no rest for me.

I faltered, fainted at my task,
　　Performed it wearily–
I had no future, lost all hope;
　　There was no rest for me.

At last, accustomed to the yoke,
　　Rest ceased to be my plea,
I grew familiar with the thought
　　That it was not for me.

But when the fabric fair on which
I worked unceasingly,
Was finished, lo, the Master cried,
"Now rest within, with Me."

Ah faithless, peevish, childish heart!
The end thou couldst not see;
The Master Builder did but plan
A nobler rest for thee!

Backsliding

All I am suffering now is just the portion
Brought on myself by falling back from Thee
My dearest Friend, in folly most astounding;
Oh can I pardoned, rescued can I be?

Canst Thou permit me to fall down before Thee,
Wilt Thou contrition give, and wilt Thou show
Once more Thy face till I again adore Thee,
Once more Thy voice may hear,
Thy grace may know?

Lord Jesus, if Thou dost, I cannot promise
Henceforth to serve and love but Thee alone;
I cannot trust myself, I am unfaithful;
Have often wandered, am to wander prone.

I only come to Thee in desperation;
Sick of myself and every word and deed;
Plead Thou my cause, Thou friend of fallen sinners,
For me Thy erring, sorrowing, creature plead.

And oh this wandering heart make strong and steadfast,
Fix Thou this will that I may rove no more;
Let me see Thee, who art of love an ocean,
Nor cast one lingering look towards earth's shore.

So Be It

So be it; 'tis Thy plan not mine,
    And being Thine is good;
My God, my will shall yield to Thine
    Ere it is understood.

So be it; I a child of dust
    Will not oppose Thy way,
Move on, mysterious Will, I trust,
    I love, and will obey.

So be it; and do Thou, my heart,
    No childish questions ask,
Thou in God's counsels hast no part,
    Crave not so hard a task.

So be it; yes, so be it, Lord,
    No word have I to say–
O be Thy gracious Name adored–
    I love and will obey.

"Nearer to Thee"

I am alone; no human eye
    Heeds where I am or what I do–
How shall I spend the time, what work
    What pastime shall I now pursue?

If Thou, dear Jesus, wert on earth
    In human form, how soon my feet
Should run to seek Thee; how my heart
    Would listen to Thy counsels sweet.

This leisure hour would soon slip by,
    If in it I might speak to Thee,
If I might tell Thee of my love,
    And know that Thou wert near to me.

But since Thou art not here on earth
In human form, yet still draw nigh
By Thy blest Spirit, let me feel
The Son of David passes by.

Give me some token that Thou still
Canst look from heavenly heights above
With the same pitying tenderness,
Which once filled earth with sacred love.

I long to feel Thee near, to know
That I a sinner, yet am Thine,
And what is more, beyond a doubt,
To know that Thou art truly mine.

To know and feel Thee just as near
As they who once embraced Thy feet,
Who oft beheld Thy sacred form,
At pleasure could their Master greet.

Ah nothing less can satisfy
The heart that hungers so for Thee,
But waking in Thy likeness, Lord,
From sin and sense forever free.

Night

Dear Lord, I do remember Thou hast said
That I may cast my every care on Thee;
But see, this deep oppression will not go,
But with its leaden hands holds fast to me.

Holds fast, and drags me down, and shuts my mouth,
Strangles the cry that fain would pierce the skies;
Helpless I lie before Thee, with no words
Upon my lips, with sad tearless eyes.

So be it, Lord; my joyous soul has need
  Of its dark days, and in this dreary night,
Roots shall strike downward, that anon shall shoot
  In rich and living branches to the light.

Oh may these branches bear some fruit for Thee,
  In grateful memory of the loving hand,
That cast me in this gloomy, cheerless spot,
  And all its dreariness and darkness planned.

Rest

Rest, weary feet!
Rest from your ceaseless wanderings,
    your travels to and fro,
The countless steps you had to take,
    fatigue to undergo.
There are no painful paths to tread,
    here is your journey's end,
The quiet grave shall welcome you
    and be to you a friend.

Rest, busy hands!
Rest from the labors that you wrought
    from dawn to set of sun,
From work that only ended
    when another was begun;
Fold them in peace and leisure now,
    they have no more to do–
Let the poor tired servants rest,
    they have been true to you.

Rest, beating heart!
Rest from thy joys tumultuous,
    from sorrow and from pain,
It shall not faint by joy consumed,
    it shall not mourn again,
Let it lie down and rest awhile,
    secure from all alarm,

This grave knows how to quiet it,
    knows how to bring it balm.

Rest, toiling brain.
Rest from the vigil that consumed,
    the nights of sleepless care,
From thoughts that tortured and condemned,
    from tasks it could not bear;
Upon this pillow, icy cold,
    within this narrow bed,
There lies no fevered, wakeful mind,
    not any aching head.

Rest, eager soul!
Thou hadst thy wings and tried them oft,
    they fluttered back to earth,
Thy pinions, not like thee, divine,
    knew not thy heavenly birth;
This grave is not thy home and end,
    mount upward and away–
Activity shall be thy rest
    from henceforth and for aye,
Thou shalt find blissful fellowship
    with souls to thine akin,
Eternal gates shall open wide
    to let the long-sought in;
Thrice blessed art thou, living soul!
    Spring homeward to thy rest,
Among the throngs that rest no more,
    and are forever blest!

Faint Not

Faint not beneath the loving Hand
    That wisely chastens thee,
Jesus will make thee understand
    Why this sharp stroke must be.

And if thy pains are long drawn out,
   Oh weary not, be strong,
Suffer in patience, Jesus' love
   Can do thy soul no wrong.

Honor the pangs that come from Him;
   Give thanks for pain and smart,
Thy groans and sighs have echoes found
   Within His sacred Heart.

Oh lonely Sufferer! Oh Lord,
   What agonies were Thine!
Give us, Thy followers, fellowship
   In sorrows so divine.

From thine own bitter cup, let all
   Thy faithful children drink,
Start we not back like coward souls,
   Nor from Thy chastening shrink.

We love Thee, choose Thee, give to us
   What first was given to Thee;
So shall we in Thy likeness grow,
   And one in heart with Thee.

Not Poor

Call me not poor; I nothing lack,
   For lo, a voice divine
Has made me feel that I am His
   And told me He is mine.

Weep not that on this weary bed,
   I long must droop and pine;
Here I have learned the peace of God,
   And know that He is mine.

Not mourn that He has torn away
My idols from their shrine;
Blest be the Hand that gave, that took,
For Jesus still is mine.

Let heaven's own radiance through the storm
Of every sorrow shine,
I heave no sigh, I shed no tear,
Am His, and He is mine.

In Grief and Shame

I lie before Thee, Lord, just where I ought
In grief and shame to lie;
I am not worthy of a glance from Thee;
Yet do not pass me by.

I have forsaken Thee, an earthly spring
Yet once again to try;
It leaves me thirsty, may I come to Thee?
O do not pass me by.

In a sad hour, a false, yet glittering prize,
Caught and enticed my eye;
I sought, and lost it, in my grief and pain,
Lord, do not pass me by.

I am so sorrowful, so sick and faint;
Long so to feel Thee nigh;
Have pity on me, tempted Son of God,
And do not pass me by.

"In Remembrance of Me"

Dear Jesus, Thou this feast hast spread,
  Invited guests are we;
We come as Thou hast bid us come,
  Thus to remember Thee.

We come from sinful thought and aim,
  More earnestly to flee;
Pardon to seek and grace to find,
  As we remember Thee.

We come to thank Thee for Thy love
  So rich, so full, so free;
To bless Thee, praise Thee, lose ourselves
  As we remember Thee.

We come to lay the burdens down
  That press most heavily;
To enter into perfect peace
  As we remember Thee.

Our penitence, our love, our hope,
  Oh condescend to see,
And let us "bear a song away"
  As we remember Thee.

"He Must Increase, But I Must Decrease"
A free translation from Lavater

Oh Jesus Christ, dwell Thou in me,
  And bid all else to vanish;
Bring my heart daily nearer Thee,
  Its sinfulness to banish.

Hover each day, in grace and might,
  Above my weak presuming,
Thy radiance swallowing up my night,
  Thy life my death consuming.

Let Thy pure sunlight on me shine,
  My soul from error freeing;
Thine all, O Christ, and nothing mine
  My soul Thee only seeing.

Draw near, I cast myself away,
  Weeping, on Thee I'm waiting,
Oh, let Thy holy will have sway,
  Thy will in mine creating.

Look gloriously forth in me,
  In wisdom, grace and gladness;
Let me Thy living image be,
  In happiness and sadness.

Make all within me new, that so
  No human weakness knowing,
Thine own devoted, loving glow
  May in my heart be glowing.

Let pride retreat, and weakness flee,
  And folly find an ending,
When towards Thy kingdom and towards Thee
  My earnest soul is tending.

And my this vain and empty I
  Be every day decreasing;
And every day that passes by
  Behold my faith increasing.

Empty self out of me each day;
  Fill with Thy presence dearer,
O Thou who over prayer hast sway,
  Be of my prayer the Hearer!

May faith in Thee my impulse prove,
  My inmost soul inspire;
Be Thou, O Christ, my joy, my love,
  My passionate desire!

Nearer to Christ

I never pressed so close to Thee, my Savior,
    But inward voices cried, Draw nearer still!
Is my heart then so large, and cannot Jesus
    With His own fulness its deep ocean fill!

What means this aching void? Is there no limit
    To the deep longing of the human soul?
Shall it know hunger and know thirst forever–
    Grasp but in fragments, never seize the whole!

Ah, childish questions! Listen to the answer;
    Great is thy heart, thy soul insatiate;
Yet has not room for Him who rules all nations,
    The coming of whose Kingdom worlds await.

Ask for a larger heart, for longings deeper;
    For richer faith with which to meet this Guest,
Who, wheresoever He finds room, will enter
    And satisfy the restless with His rest.

Walking With God

He walks with God! Enough for me
That this I in my brother see;
I ask not what his rank, or name,
Whether obscure, or rich in fame,
Who fall before him, or who rise;
If he be ignorant or wise.

He walks with God! To Him allied,
He presses closely to His side;
No more of him I ask to know,
But gladly I with him will go;
My brother he, my dearest friend;
With him I would a life-time spend.

He walks with God! Oh, kinship sweet,
For saints and angels only, meet,
How steadfast and how true the heart
That from its Master will not part!
Though never warm or true to me,
I love it, Lord, for loving Thee!

He walks with God! Nor ever heeds
Over what heights his pathway leads.
Or where to valley dips the road;
Enough for him to be with God;
Enough that earthly joy or pain
Tempting, can only tempt in vain.

He walks with God! I lift mine eye
And see what fields before him lie;
The river clear, the pasture green;
What matters what may intervene?
Lord, when he is at home, with Thee
O let his mantle fall on me!

A Cup of Water

Dear Jesus, where wert Thou when I refused
   To give a cup of water for Thy sake?
Where did I part with Thee, how did I dare
   A single step in my own strength to take?

This shows me what I am; it shows that deep
   In my heart's core the love of self still lies;
I have no goodness, in my own conceit
   Oh let me never, never more be wise!

And wilt Thou condescend the cup to fill
   My sinful hands put by, and may the lip
I would not moisten, taste Thy living draught,
   And evermore its strength and sweetness sip!

Angel's Food

Thou canst eat angels' food,
    my soul, turn from earth's husks away,
They are not fitted for thy wants,
    thy hunger can not stay;
The servants in thy Father's house
    have better bread than thine
Who art His own adopted one,
    why then mid plenty pine?

Thou canst of living waters drink,
    why turn to earthly springs
That at the fountainhead are dry,
    amid inferior things;
Come to the crystal rivers pure
    that flow through pastures green,
That make their gladsome sparkling way,
    the smitten rocks between.

Thou canst inhale, thou pilgrim soul,
    the atmosphere of heaven,
By Him who deals in bounteous gifts
    its fulness shall be given,
Then wilt thou in the mortal strife,
    in human weakness, dare
To breathe amid the vapors foul
    of earth's sin-tainted air?

Ah foolish soul! ah childish soul!
    Ah soul on ruin bent,
This world is not thy home,
    thy rest, thou are in banishment;
Build not with too much care thy nest;
    thou shalt be stripped and peeled,
Made hungry, thirsty, sick and faint,
    ere thy disease is healed.

Yet fear thou not and falter not,
   despise not thou the way;
The long, dark night shall usher in
   joy's own resplendent day;
Soon safe within thy Father's house
   by Him thou shalt be fed,
Shalt drink His wine, sit at His feast,
   and taste the living bread.

What matters then the rage of thirst,
   the gnaw of hunger's pang,
The cry for air that from thy heart
   in stifling terror rang?
What matter that thou hast not
   where on earth to build a nest?
The day is brighter after night,
   toil only sweetens rest.

Testimony

How gladly would Thy children, Lord,
   In goodly company,
Unite to sound Thy praises out,
   And testify of Thee.

If we oft times in silence sit,
   Thou who our hearts dost know,
Seest a love that finds no words
   And tears that do not flow.

There rests upon our mortal tongues,
   Sometimes a secret spell,
It is not coldness that is mute,
   But love that loves too well.

We thank, we bless Thee, that to Thee
   This is no sinful mood,
That by the depths that dwell in Thine
   Our hearts are understood.

Search us and try us, not alone
 Our sinfulness to see,
But to detect the love that longs
 To testify of Thee.

"At Evening Time There Shall Be Light"

At evening time there shall be light!
 Yes, when the night draws nigh,
When shadows lengthen, and the sun
 Is parting from the sky;
When the warm air grows chill, and earth
 Lies in obscurity;

There shall be light! A light unseen
 Amid the glare of day,
It shall illume the lonely path
 Through which thy footsteps stray,
To guide thee, lure thee, cheer thee on
 Amid the darkest way.

There shall be light! As tender hands
 Light children to their bed,
So shall thou just as lovingly,
 As tenderly be led,
And shown upon what pillow, thou
 Mayst lay thy weary head.

There shall be light! Yet faith's bright eye
 Alone that light can see;
Can take from death its chill, its gloom,
 And lend it ecstasy;
Look up! And see the risen Christ
 Shine, like the sun, for Thee!

A Cold Heart

I know that I love Thee my Savior,
Yet my heart lies as cold as a stone,
I have not the strength to grow warmer,
Nor life enough for Thee to groan.

I know that I love Thee, my Savior,
Yet veiled and unsought is Thy face,
I see not, I hear not, I feel not
Of what I once knew of Thy grace.

I know that I love Thee, my Savior,
Though withered and stupid and dead,
Though the shower of blessing is failing,
And all that has cheered me has fled.

I know that I love Thee, my Savior!
Away then with fear and with doubt,
Let me rest in this sorrowful prison,
Till Thou Thyself callest me out.

Satisfied

"I shall be satisfied when I awake with Thy likeness." Ps. 17:15

What shall I find in heaven? The faces dear
Upon whose love and smiles I feasted here?
Shall I rejoice that naught can there divide
United hearts, and so be satisfied?

What shall I do in heaven? Shall I be blest
With a long luxury and endless rest?
Conflict and labor over, shall I ride
Through seas untroubled, and be satisfied?

What shall I be in heaven? A messenger
Passing from sainted ones to those who err

And suffer still on earth? Mid fields so wide,
Shall I, who love to work, be satisfied?

I know not, care not; when life's fetters break,
When from death's blessed restful sleep I wake,
Whate'er Thy love withhold, or may provide,
Being like Thee, I shall be satisfied!

Joint Heir With Christ
"It is enough for the disciple that he be as his Lord."

What aileth thee, my heart? Thy lamentations
  Fill all the air, yet Jesus draweth nigh;
This is His gift, the sorrow thou deplorest;
  He chose this anguish, counted out each sigh;
  The Son of David would not pass thee by.

Wounded, imprisoned heart, He comes for healing
  From thy captivity to set thee free,
Thy blinded eyes He comes Himself to open,
  The sore, sad weight to render sweet to thee;
  He passes by, and thou His face canst see.

Thou falterest, my heart? Then lay thy burden
  At His dear feet, who came the cross to bear,
Give Him this grief; upon the Man of sorrows
  Lay thou thy sorrows, lay thine every care,
  And overwhelm Him with thy deep despair.

For as his Lord shall not be the disciple;
  Christ may endure the cross and bear the shame;
He may walk homeless, sleep without a pillow,
  And He who for our sakes a Man became,
  Have scorn and anger heaped upon His name.

But thou, self-lover, choosest ease and leisure,
  Thou with this Man of sorrows hast no part;
Thou must have home and friends and reputation,

A life of peace, an unencumbered heart,
Pleasure's bright sparkle, not affliction's smart!

For shame! For shame! Arise in strength courageous,
Bear thine own burden though it be with tears;
Follow the Master, imitate His patience,
If need be, follow three and thirty years
Mid poverty, mid loneliness and fears.

It is enough that of His grief partaker,
Thou shalt with Him in all His glory share;
Shalt own the love that meted out thy sorrows,
Proclaim His praise, His faithfulness declare,
And with Him enter heaven His joint heir!

God's Way

Dear Lord, I often tell Thee that I fain
Would give some great and costly gift to Thee;
Yea, I have almost courted loss and pain,
If I thereby might proved and humbled be.

And now the Hand that I have asked to take
From out my store some dear, some precious thing,
Does not disdain this bruis-ed heart to break,
To get possession of its offering.

Yes, blood-drops ooze from many a rent that Thou
Thyself has torn, and I am faint and sore;
I feel a death-like moisture on my brow
And on my dizzy brain wild voices roar.

Bur oh I waver not! Thou knowest well
I meant that Thou shouldst take me at my word,
The bitter waves of anguish rise and swell,
But heed them not, my Master and my Lord.

Keep what Thou hast in wise and tender grace,
  Snatched from my deepest depths, nor left to me
Option or choice; love shines upon Thy face,
  Thou knowest best what I can spare for Thee.

But oh, by all this pain, this bleeding heart,
  Subdue, control, beat down and lay me low;
New knowledge of Thyself to me impart,
  Jesus, my Savior, let me learn to know.

I smart, I writhe, I bleed–and still I cry–
  Lo that Thou hast is Thine, is mine no more;
Thou Master of my treasures are, and I
  In this new poverty Thy name adore!

Prayer

My soul is weak, its purposes are poor,
Of nothing in itself it can be sure,
Nor knows that to the end it can endure;
      And so I love to pray.

My heart is cold, it does not always beat
With glowing love to Jesus, as is meet,
Nor always run His blessed form to greet;
      And so I love to pray.

My mind is ignorant and dark; I know
So little of the way in which to go,
My progress is so tedious and so slow,
      And so I love to pray.

For praying, I can feel that God is strong,
That in my weakness I to Him belong,
That He can nothing do or false or wrong–
      Dearly I love to pray!

And my cold heart grows warmer as it tells
Its story pitiful, with love it swells
To Him who unseen ever near it dwells,
    And so I love to pray.

And in communing with the great All-Wise,
What scales drop off from my poor, blinded eyes!
What gracious lessons He to me supplies!
    Ah Lord! I love to pray!

Where Is He?

Oh where is He for whom my soul is pining,
    For whom I yearn, and thirst, and pant, and pray?
Around His empty cross my arms I'm twining,
    What daring hand has borne His form away?

He is my soul's beloved, my heart's treasure–
    With Him this weary world could restful be;
Without Him language is too poor to measure,
    How desolate, how homeless it would be.

Say you the Lord has left His cross behind Him
    For you to hang on, and from hence is gone?
Gone? Whither? But my heart shall go and find Him,
    Not linger here, defrauded and forlorn.

Tell me, how went He? Point in the direction
    And I will follow wheresoe'er He leads;
All paths are one to passionate affection–
    That neither time, nor pain, nor peril heeds.

What say you? He has homeward gone, and left me
    To follow thither? Gladly, Lord, I come!
I knew Thou hadst not of Thyself bereft me–
    One moment more and I too am at home!

What hands invisible are these that hold me,
  And beat me back, and will not let me go?
Cease to oppose, presume not to enfold me–
  I fly to Him I love, to Him I know.

I may not, say ye? May not hope to clasp Him
  Save in the ministry of pain and loss,
My loving arms may never reach to grasp Him
  Save through His martyrdom and on His cross!

Quick with the nails then! Spare not for my crying
  Where my Beloved hung let me too hang–
In this sweet agony death is not dying–
  The pang that bears to Him, it is no pang!

The Mother

As I have seen a mother bend
  With aching, bleeding heart,
O'er lifeless limbs and lifeless face–
  So have I had to part.

With the sweet prattler at my knee,
  The baby from my breast,
And on the lips so cold in death,
  Such farewell kisses prest.

If I should live a thousand years
  Time's hand cannot efface,
The features painted on my heart
  Of each beloved face.

If I should bathe in endless seas
  They could not wash away
The memory of these children's forms;
  How fresh it is to-day.

Ah, how my grief has taught my heart
  To feel another's woe!
With what a sympathetic pang
  I watch the tear-drops flow!

Dear Jesus! must Thou take our lambs,
  Our cherished lambs away?
Thou hast so many, we so few—
  Canst Thou not let them stay?

Must the round limbs we love so well,
  Grow stiff and cold in death?
Must all our loveliest flowerets fall
  Before his icy breath?

Nay Lord, but it is hard, is hard—
  Oh give us faith to see,
That grief, not joy, is best for us
  Since it is sent by Thee.

And oh, by all our mortal pangs
  Hear Thou the mother's plea—
Be gracious to the darling ones
  We've given back to Thee.

Let them not miss the mother's love,
  The mother's fond caress;
Gather them to Thy gentle breast
  In faithful tenderness.

Oh lead them into pastures green,
  And unto living springs;
Gather them in Thine arms, and shield
  Beneath Thy blessed wings.

Ah, little reck we that we weep,
  And wring our empty hands;—
Blessed, thrice blessed are infant feet,
  That walk Immanuel's lands!

Blessed the souls that ne'er shall know
    Of sin the mortal taint,
The hearts that ne'er shall swell with grief
    Or utter a complaint!

Brief pangs for us, long joy for them!
    Thy holy Name we bless,
We could not give them up to Thee,
    Lord, if we loved them less!

"Oh Come Thou Down to Me, Or Take Me Up to Thee!"

I would be with Thee, dearest Lord,
    I long Thy face to see,
I long that each succeeding day
    should bring me nearer Thee;
Wilt Thou come down to dwell with me,
    wilt Thou with me abide;
Wilt Thou go with me where I go,
    be ever at my side?

Thy home is with the humble, Lord;
    that blessed truth I know;
But cannot change my heart myself,
    do Thou, then, make it so;
Oh come, my Savior, come to me,
    it is not life to live,
Unless thy presence fills my soul,
    except Thyself Thou give.

Or, if Thou canst not come to me,
    a weak, a sinful child,
If Thou, alas, dost find in me
    no temple undefiled,
Oh then my gracious Lord, send down
    a messenger for me,

And strip my sinfulness away
and take me up to Thee.

I care not where I find Thee, Lord,
whether or here or there,
I only know I want to find
and love Thee, everywhere;
This world with all its tears and groans,
would be my chosen place,
If Thou shouldst plan it for the scene
in which to show Thy face.

And heaven with all its peace and rest,
would be no heaven to me,
If I might dwell forever there,
without a glimpse of Thee;
It is not life, or life's best joys,
it is not heaven I want,
But oh, Thou risen Christ, for Thee,
for Thee alone, I pant!

"Dying, Yet Behold We Live"

A ship, full laden left her native port,
To plough the waves, and seek another clime;
Her sails were set, and gallant ranks of men,
If the wind failed, would with their oars keep time.

Her port she left, but on a troubled main,
Her every sinew, every nerve, she strained;
Yet wooed the breezes, spread her sails in vain–
She sped not on her way, nor land she gained.

Then rose the pilot, "Heed my words," he cried
"Too many a weighty gift this ship ye gave;
Cast this and that away, and she shall ride
Lightly, and unencumbered, o'er the wave."

With niggard hand, reluctantly they drew
  Some trifles from her breast, and in the sea
They one by one these secret treasures threw,
  And saw them sink in its immensity.

Yet still, as if held back by leaden hands,
  The ship no progress made, and so once more,
The pilot, working her from off the sands,
  Made the same plaint his voice had made before.

Then one by one her treasures left her deck
  To be by yawning, briny jaws consumed,
And mid fierce winds and storms, an empty wreck,
  Went staggering into port, condemned and doomed.

And yet the pilot from the master won
  Plaudits and welcomes that his zeal repaid,
For on his ear there fell the glad well done,
  Who, faithful to his trust, no trust betrayed.

Thus, O my soul, thy Pilot made thy way
  Straight to the haven where thou fain wouldst be;
Nor feared to rob thee, cut thy spars away,
  Knowing the Master only cared for thee.

For thee, dismantled, empty, good for naught,
  For thee, who unto him no treasure bore;
Then ride at anchor, tempest-tossed, distraught,
  For thou has touched at an eternal shore!

Only Jesus

From the German

Jesus, Jesus, only Jesus,
  Shall become my wish and aim;
Now I make a sacred promise
  That our wills shall be the same;
For my heart in sweet accord,
Cries, "Thy will be done," dear Lord.

There is One whom I am loving,
  Loving early, loving late;
He to me my all has given,
  All to Him I consecrate,
Thou Thy blood on me hast poured,
Let Thy will be done, dear Lord!

If what seems to be a blessing
  Is not chosen, planned by Thee,
Oh deprive me of it, rather
  Give me what is good for me;
Still Thy name shall be adored,
Where Thy will despoils me, Lord!

Let Thy will be done within me,
  Through me, by me, ever done,
Done in life, in joy, in sorrow,
  Till the victory is won.
Dying, be in me restored,
When, how, where Thou wilt, dear Lord!

"Your Darling Sleeps"

A very free translation from the German

Your darling sleeps; bid not his slumbers cease,
  Permit this sweet repose;
Lying among the flowers, and full of peace,
  He says, to soothe your woes–
I lie enfolded in delightful rest,
The lines have fall'n to me among the blest–
  Your darling sleeps.

Your darling sleeps; all wearied out with play
  And satisfied with joy;
Forgotten now is what beguiled the day,
  Forgotten festival, and book, and toy,
The treasures that he loved can charm no more,
For his young feet have climbed to Eden's door–
  Your darling sleeps.

Your darling sleeps; his day of life was gay
    And rich in joyous hours;
A sparkling brook that made its gladsome way
    Through fields of blooming flowers;
Sorrow nor knew him or his presence sought,
With him not death itself in conflict wrought–
    Your darling sleeps.

Your darling sleeps; how blessed and how sure,
    On the good Shepherd's arm!
His childish heart from sinful stain made pure,
    Death could not do him harm;
Compassed with holy nurture, holy care,
His dying pillow was parental prayer–
    Your darling sleeps.

Your darling sleeps; and so he sleeps away
    Life's bitter, threatening hours;
Know'st thou, oh mother, what conceal-ed lay,
    Amid its adverse powers?
Now wintry storms for him may vainly beat,
Vainly may summer scorch with fervid heat,
    Your darling sleeps.

Your darling sleeps; but for a single night,
    Whose gloomy shades must flee;
And when the day dawns forth with rosy light,
    That will a morning be!
The Man of sorrows, pitying your grief,
Will come, as once of old, to your relief–
    Your darling sleeps.

Your darling sleeps; and now the parting kiss
    Upon his white lips press;
O mother-heart, through such an hour as this
    Christ pity your distress!
He walks upon life's billows, and He will
Allay the storm and all its moanings still–
    Your darling sleeps.

Your darling sleeps; close to Thy tender breast,
　　Good Shepherd, clasp our trust!
Ye stars, look kindly on his place of rest,
　　And guard his precious dust!
Ye winds float round him on a gentle wing,
Ye flowers, a lavish fragrance o'er him fling!
　　Our darling sleeps.

Nearer

　　Oh Jesus, draw nearer,
　　And make Thyself dearer,
I yearn, I am yearning for Thee;
　　Come take for Thy dwelling,
　　The heart that is swelling
With longings Thy beauty to see!

　　How languid and weary,
　　How lonely and dreary,
The days when Thou hidest Thy face;
　　How sorrow and sadness
　　Are turned into gladness,
By a glimpse of its love and its grace.

　　Come nearer, come nearer,
　　And make Thyself dearer,
Thou joy, Thou delight of my heart.
　　Close, close to Thee pressing
　　I long for Thy blessing,
I cannot without it depart.

Sorrow

I have known Sorrow; I have been acquainted
　　With her pale face; her voice, her footsteps known,
Oft uninvited she has crossed my threshold,
　　　　To speak with me alone.

I loved her not! I gave to her no welcome;
   Asked not her errand, closed to her my heart;
With chilling words, and with a face averted,
     I urged her to depart.

She went, but came again; as a dove flutters
   Above some dear retreat, she oft returned;
I heard her wings but offered her no shelter,
     Her coming flight I spurned.

At last, by my repelling frowns unwearied,
   Again she ventured nigh, and thus she spake:
"I come from One thou lovest!" showed her tokens,
     Grew welcome, for His sake.

Thenceforth she sat my guest, revered and honored
   And her stern face unlovely ceased to be.
When life interpreting, she sat beside me,
     Made Christ more dear to me.

And yet her presence drove from out my threshold,
   The treasures that His hand in bounty gave;
Groans wrung she from me, as I knelt in anguish
     At the relentless grave.

Upon the rock of sore suspense she laid me,
   Not once, but often, tore me limb from limb;
And when I shrank, and wept, and cried for mercy,
     She pointed but to Him.

And so by turns sore-smitten, soothed, instructed,
   I sit at her dear feet, and smile on her,
Who came on wings of love to scourge and prove me–
     Christ's precious messenger!

"God Loves to be Longed For,
He Loves to be Sought"

Lord, is this true? Ah, canst Thou really love
  These longings in the soul, that only tell
Of emptiness, of depths unsatisfied,
  Of waves that on a boundless ocean swell?

And dost Thou love me when I only seek,
  Yet do not find Thee? When I go astray,
And stumble blindly onward in the dark,
  And cannot see, but only feel, my way?

Ah! I am truly longing! Both my arms
  Are stretched, with speechless yearnings, after Thee;
Naught else have I to give Thee, dearest Lord,
  No grace, no beauty, canst Thou see in me.

And I am truly seeking! All day long,
  In silent thought and prayer, to Thee I turn;
At home, abroad, alone, or in the crowd,
  I strive to find Thee, strive Thy paths to learn.

Longing and seeking! These two words declare
  All that I am and hope for; great the thought
That Thou canst love this longing, love the heart
  That, while it seeks Thee, in itself is naught.

Jesus, dear Master, give to me the power
  Thy name to love, to honor and adore;
I long for Thee! I seek Thee! Let me long,
  And let me ever seek Thee, more and more.

Broken to be Mended

Suggested by the remark of a bereaved friend:
"We cannot be mended unless we are broken."

Jesus, our tears with blessed smiles are blending,
For Thou who knowest how our hearts to break,
Knowest the happy secret of their mending,
And we rejoice in sorrow for Thy sake.

Yes, break us all to pieces, at Thy pleasure,
For the poor fragments can be joined by Thee;
Snatch from us, if Thou wilt, our every treasure!
Possessing Thee we never poor can be.

There is a sweetness in a spirit broken,
That lofty souls attain not–cannot know;
To such a heart Thy promises are spoken,*
Thou hast a solace for its silent woe.

And when our weary days on earth are ended,
And from its agitations we are free,
We shall rejoice that we were broken, mended,
By Thine own skillful hand, dear Lord, by Thee.

* Psalm 51:17

"That I May Win Christ"

Dear Jesus, every morning's light
Brings a new love to Thee;
Each makes of Thee a new delight,
New strength, new joy to me.

I want to give myself away
In bonds as fresh, as new;
Let a new love be born each day,
A love more deep, more true.

I would forget, in pressing on,
　All that is left behind.
A changeless goal has not been won,
　Not yet my Lord I find.

The goal is changing! With each morn
　There springs a higher aim,
With each are deeper longings born,
　Life's object not the same.

Thou dost, with Thine inspiring grace,
　My halting steps allure;
I know that I shall see Thy face,
　To win Thee I am sure.

Oh, who, such blessed race to run,
　Would not each morning rise,
Knowing that God's eternal Son
　Shall be the victor's prize?

An Angel Smiling

Dear Lord, into my heart, already sore,
　　Sharp, piercing thorns are pressing;
I recognize the Hand that oft before,
　　Has, in such guise, sent blessing.

I shrink not from this pain; my hands clasp Thine
　　To help it pierce the deeper;
I know these wounds are precious and divine,
　　I am a happy weeper.

For oh! I weep not that I smart and bleed,
　　But that my patient willing,
Falls in with Thy dear will in thought and deed,
　　And every pain is stilling.

I weep because Thy will has grown so sweet,
 That even a thorn brings gladness;
That all which humbles, drives me to Thy feet,
 Is precious sadness.

So pierce, so wound, my Master, for this heart
 Against Thy thorns is pressing,
Rejoicing in their pain, and in their smart,
 Thy tenderness confessing.

Oh, blessed Will of God! It sorrow daunts
 While of its sting beguiling;
And where a torment only stood, it plants
 An angel smiling.

Yearning

How long it is since I have seen Thy face,
 And how I yearn to see it! Dearest Lord,
I dare not ask to see it, though such grace
 Transporting joy and gladness would afford.

Let me be patient in this long delay;
 If I have lost Thee, all the fault is mine–
Perhaps when Thou wert near I turned away–
 And lost the light that would upon me shine.

Forgive the folly, and forgive the sin–
 It was not wilful,–how it came and when–
At what vile door the Tempter entered in,
 I do not know; oh turn him out again.

For I am very weary, very sad–
 Life is so desolate afar from Thee;
I miss the joys sublime that once I had;
 I long, I yearn for Thy lost sympathy.

The Christian Life

Wouldst thou take the gauge of the Christian life,
    And measure it out by rule?
Wouldst thou circumscribe it, and plane it down,
    And define it in some school?

But there is no plummet can reach its depths;
    No foot that can scale its heights;
No painter its varying features paint,
    No poet its pure delights.

Its mystical grace is grace of its own,
    And springs from a mystic Fount;
Now in the valley it makes its way,
    And now it ascends the mount.

Believe in it, trust it, with all thy soul,
    And love it with all thine heart;
Seek it where others have sought it out,
    And learn what they can impart.

But he who knows, and who loves it best,
    Will ever declare to thee,
It is all a wonder, a miracle,
    And always a mystery!

He Is Mine

O Christ, I yearn for more of Thee;
Reveal, reveal Thyself to me,
    And satisfy this heart
    That would be Thine alone.
I want Thee wholly, not in part,
I want to know that mine Thou art,
    To know as I am known;
Within this breast Thy love has glowed,
Oh, come and make it Thine abode.

When I can see Thy face divine,
A sunbeam seems on me to shine;
    And if Thou turn away,
    Joy ceases to be joy.
Night's blackest darkness stifles day,
I am of restless grief the prey,
    Its idle sport and toy;
I know, for I have tasted this–
Have missed Thee, mourned Thee, felt Thy bliss.

Oh, Thou my Life, my Joy, my End,
Dearer than any earthly friend,
    How can I speak Thy love?
    What say I have not said?
When streaming eyes have looked above,
These hands held fast the heavenly Dove,
    That pleaded in my stead:
Has not Thy penetrating glance
Read that which knows no utterance?

And yet I yearn to love Thee more,
With saintly rapture to adore
    Thy dear and precious Name,
    That must be dearer yet;
I come Thy promises to claim,
Thy love my boldness will not blame,
    Thy heart my plea forget;
Let praises be my every breath,
My hourly life of self the death.

Thou hast lit up with ardor rare
Some hidden souls, Thy special care;
    Make me to them akin!
    Give me what Thou to them hast given,
Their high devotion let me win,
Their calm dominion over sin,
    Making of earth a heaven–
The wondrous and mysterious grace
Of ever looking on Thy face!

They went to meet Thee by a way
That pilgrim feet still tread to-day,
    And counting all things dross
    Save Him they in long patience sought;
Let me press on through pain and loss,
Bending beneath my Master's cross,
    Learning as they were taught;
Jesus, Beloved of my heart,
I feel Thine Answer—mine Thou art!

"Am I My Brother's Keeper?"

Am I my brother's keeper? Yes,
    I owe him love and care;
The word of counsel and of cheer;
    The power of earnest prayer.

When fierce temptation shakes his soul,
    My strength should be his stay;
When flattering voices lure to sin,
    My form should bar his way.

When sickness lays him low, my time,
    My faithful ministries,
My health, my courage, all I have,
    Should patiently be his.

And when his day of life grows dark,
    And tears his eye bedim,
Mine is the heart to feel his grief,
    To sympathize with him.

My brother's keeper, then, am I;
    O Christ, within me shine,
That mine may be the sacred joy
    To help him to be Thine.

Alone With God

Into my closet fleeing, as the dove
    Doth homeward flee,
I haste away to ponder o'er Thy love
    Alone with Thee!

In the dim wood, by human ear unheard,
    Joyous and free,
Lord! I adore Thee, feasting on Thy word
    Alone with Thee!

Amid the busy city, thronged and gay,
    But One I see,
Tasting sweet peace, as unobserved I pray
    Alone with Thee!

O happy life! Life hid with Christ in God
    So making me,
At home, and by the wayside, and abroad,
    Alone with Thee!

It Cannot Last

Weary now it is, and must be,
    All my sky is overcast;
But no cloud can be eternal,
    This one cannot always last!

Drearily the storm is beating,
    Chilling rain is falling fast;
I am wet, and cold, and cheerless;
    But it cannot always last!

Walls of granite, stern, forbidding,
    Separate me from the past,
That was erst so glad, so joyous;–
    But they cannot always last!

And what sorrows lie before me
In the future drear and vast;
Ah, I know not! But it cheers me
That they cannot always last!

Something For Christ

Something for Thee! Lord, let this be
Thy choice for me from day to day;
The life I live it is not mine,
Thy will, my will, have made it Thine!
Oh let me do in Thine own way,
Something for Thee!

Something for Thee! What shall it be?
Speak, Lord, Thy waiting servant hears,
Is it to do some mighty deed?
Is it some multitude to feed?
Is it to do mid pains and fears,
Something for Thee?

Something for Thee! I do not see
A coming battle for my King,
I only see a little cup–
With water haste to fill it up:
Thy love will own this trivial thing,
Something for Thee!

Something for Thee! From self I flee,
What wilt Thou, Master, from me still?
With eager heart I stand and wait,
Longing for work, or small or great:
Let me be doing as Thy will,
Something for Thee!

Something for Thee! On bended knee,
Unseen, unknown by mortal eye,
My soul for other souls shall plead–

As Thou for me didst intercede.
Thy love can own a tear, a sigh,
Something for Thee!

Something for Thee! Yet if for me
It is a useless, crippled hand,
Let perfect patience mark my way:
Since they who silently obey
Are doing as Thy wisdom planned,
Something for Thee!

Forgive !

Dear Lord, forgive
The evil passions that within me live,
Make my whole heart
Of Thine a part,
And let Thy Spirit rule and reign in me
That I may perfect be, complete in Thee.

I do hate sin
And all the wretched work it does within;
I cannot rest,
When in my breast,
I see its motions and its mad desires,
Oh purge me, Lord, e'en though it be through fires.

The Pilgrim

From the German of Schiller
Read this poem of Schiller's with that Name, which is above every name,
as its solution. "The there" is "here" — Mrs. Charles

Life was only in its spring-tide,
When to wander forth inclined,
Youth I left with all its gladness
In my father's house behind.

Joyful, full of faith, my birthright,
    All I had I tossed away,
Then a pilgrim's staff inclasping,
    Childish folly won the day.

For a mighty hope inspired me,
    Faith clasped hands with vague desire
"On," I cried, "the way is open,
    Ever upward, ever higher!

"On, until a golden portal
    Shall to enter welcome thee:
There the earthly shall be heavenly,
    Heavenly and immortal be."

It was night, and came the morning,
    Never, never stood I still;
But there yet remained concealed
    What I wanted, what would will.

Mountains rose to bar my progress,
    Rivers deep my way withstood,
Over gulfs I built me causeways,
    Passed in safety, bridged the flood.

To a river's shore arriving,
    Whose wide current eastward prest
Full of faith, I gladly cast me
    Straight into its flowing breast.

Making me its sport, it bore me
    Onward to a mighty sea:
Naught but empty space before me,
    All I aimed for fled from me.

Ah! no bridge will lead me thither;
    Heaven will not to earth come near
But forever smile beyond me,
    While the *There* is never *Here*.

Work

"Lord, what would'st Thou have me to do?"

Lord, send me work to do for Thee
    Let not a single day
Be spent in waiting on myself,
    Or wasted pass away.

And teach me how to work for Thee;
    Thy Spirit, Lord, impart,
That I may serve Thee less from fear
    Than from a loving heart.

And bless the work I do for Thee,
    Or I shall toil in vain;
Mine be the hand to drop the seed;
    Thine to send sun and rain.

Thrice happy he who works for Thee;
    Thou grantest him the grace,
When he takes home his work to see
    The Master, face to face.

Jesus, Be All

O Lord, I know that Thou wilt give to me
    All that I really want;
And yet with heart insatiate and athirst
    For more of Thee I pant.

Bid me long on: help me to strive and pray
    For I would rather kneel
Rent by conflicting wants, than never thirst
    For Thee, my Lord, to feel.

Give me the prayer of faith, that must prevail!
    Dictate what my poor heart

Shall say to Thee, and how it shall be said,
    Jesus, till mine Thou art!

Come to me with my earliest waking thought,
    Be with me where I go;
Be my last thought at night, and in my dreams
    Thy blessed presence show.

I am so weak, so helpless, Thou so strong;
    Oh, do not let me fall!
My self-despair alone must plead my cause
    Jesus, be Thou mine all!

Complete in Christ

"Ye are complete in Him."

Complete in Him! Oh Lord, I flee,
Laden with this great thought, to Thee
With tears and smiles contending, cry,
Are words like these for such as I?

Complete in Him! No word of mine
Is needed, Lord, to perfect Thine;
Wise Master-Builder, let Thy hand
Fashion the fabric Thou hast planned.

Complete in Him! I nothing bring,
Am an imperfect, useless thing;
But human eyes shall joy to see
What God's dear hand shall add to me.

Complete in Him! Oh, longed-for day,
When my poor, sinful heart can say,
Naught in myself, for ruin meet,
In Jesus Christ I stand complete!

"Joy Unspeakable"

The Christian life! What is its explanation?
  Is it a law of discipline and pain?
So stern a law that hearts can never carol
  A cheerful, gladsome strain?

Is it set only to a cadence mournful?
  A Miserere its peculiar song?
Surely we ever hear it, often vainly
  For Jubilates long.

Man's grief is sacred, yet he sometimes tells it
  But of his deeper joy he cannot speak;
He struggles in its mystery, and to paint it
  Finds human words too weak.

The shallow brook, that its own way is taking,
  Sings songs incessant, as it onward goes;
It has no depths, no waves, no hidden secrets;
  It has no ebbs and flows.

We hear the ocean moaning, sighing ever,
  We hear its restless tossings and its roar;
But of the "central peace" within its bosom,
  It never tells us more.

Like it, majestic, human joy is speechless;
  Like it, yet more, the joy divine is mute;
Speech may be "silvern," but a "golden silence"
  Is rapture's attribute.

Look for the soul whose glance is ever upward,
  Who sees the living Christ, who knows the grace
Of His mysterious friendship; loves Him, trust Him;
  Speaks to Him, face to face:

And you have found a soul, that though it utter
  Oft times a groan, and oft times sheds a tear,

Knows of a bliss whose language is transcendent,
   And cannot reach the ear.

Thrice blessed soul! It cannot tell its story—
   Cannot, to mortal ear, its depths betray;
But it shall tell it, giving Christ the glory,
   In His effulgent Day!

The Cry of the Young Wife

I.

What o'clock is it, Nurse? Just one?
Why, I thought it was four;
That must me moonlight, then,
lying, so white on the floor.
Ah, what long nights!
And I have not been sleeping at all,
But lying here watching your shadow
nod this way and that, on the wall.

II.

Wet my lips, Nurse; give me drink;
put some ice to my head;
No, not there—here on my forehead!
oh, how you're shaking the bed!
Oh, that I lay like the moonlight
so cold and so white,
But I'm burning with fever,
and tired, so tired to-night!

III.

In the morning I sigh for the evening;
at night I pine for the day.
All my young life-blood is scorching
and drying away.
Well, let it dry!
For my life it is nothing to me,
At best 'tis a fetter,
and I only long to be free.

IV.

The child, do you say? Nay,
don't talk to me of the child!
Lay more ice on my forehead;
be quiet, and don't look so wild.
Best for the stream at its fountain
to fail and to dry,
Best for the child with its young
little mother to die.

V.

For I am so young! I'm so young!
Oh, Nurse, don't you know
What a happy young creature
I was only four weeks ago?
He called me his darling, his plaything,
his baby—but nay,
I'm his widow—do you hear?
I am his widow, to-day.

VI.

I always thought widows were old;
wore stiff caps and gray curls;
Never dreamed that they ever were
made of young girls!
But I'm a young girl, and
my Philip was only a boy—
Brilliant and handsome.
Why, just to behold him was joy!

VII.

Why did I let him go forth
to that terrible fight?
They say it was all for his country;
that he died for the triumph of right.
Well, let the country rejoice.
It has snatched my love from my side,
And made me a widow
when I was scarcely a bride.

VIII.

Do you say it's the fever
that makes all my talking so wild?
That, perhaps, I could cry and get eased
if I would but look at my child?
Nay, nothing can give me ease now
till my hands you enfold,
And lay me down under the moonlight,
as white and as cold.

THE SONG OF THE YOUNG MOTHER

IX.

Ah, my own baby! I love thee,
I love thee at last!
The tempest of sorrow is over,
the night of my anguish is past!
Come, to my heart, thou bright creature!
closer, ah, closer my boy!
The world it no longer is empty,
it is brimming, is brimming with joy!

X.

Ah, my own baby! My darling!
Thy father's own glorious child!
Radiant in beauty thou art,
and, like him, undefiled;
All the mad love that I gave him
I pour out upon thee;
The world it no longer is empty;
but the fulness of fulness to me!

Sings–We'll grow up together, my baby,
    Thou and I together;
    We'll go hopping from bough to bough,
    Little birds of a feather!
    And we will play
    In fragrant hay,

And berries sweet
Together eat;
Thou'lt forget I'm thy little mother–
I'll make believe thou art my little brother!
Thou shalt be all in all to me,
I will be all in all to thee.
And, by-and-by, when thou art a man,
I'll be just as young as I can;
Never maiden, never a bride,
Shall steal my darling away from my side
A soldier's death thou shalt never die,
In a soldier's grave thou shalt never lie;
But bright and joyful thy life shall be,
Thou shalt be all in all to me,
And I will be all in all to thee!

HER SIGH

XI.

Down 'mid high grass
a mother-bird built her a nest;
I was that bird;
and my nestling it lies there at rest!
Was it long years ago–
was it but yesterday, say?
That laying him down there I left him,
and went on my way?

XII.

Sorrow has sought me and found me;
sorrow has silvered my hair;
At my table he sits my sole guest;
facing me solemnly there;
He has stolen my youth and my laughter;
stolen my life and my joy,
Snatched away husband and lover,
seized on my beautiful boy.

XIII.

Ah, I was joyous and thoughtless;
evil and danger defied,
Forth from gay childhood
I ran to the life of a bride.
I must have something to love;
on something must pour out my heart:
Little recked I of trouble,
little of thorn and of smart.

XIV.

And then they must kill him,
my husband, my lover, my all!
Shivered in fragments my heart
with the same fatal ball!
Shivered in fragments,
and frozen and lifeless it lay,
Whose were the hands that its warmth
to restore could assay!

XV.

Thine, my own baby! None other!
Ah, the first wakings to joy,
Under the touch of thy fingers,
my darling, my beautiful boy!
Green grew the earth 'neath my feet,
blue the sky over my head!
Of one idol bereft, in my heart
I enthroned thee instead.

XVI.

So the new current of life
went babbling along,
Sparkling and gleesome,
and full of its youth and its song;
We had not a moment for sadness,
never a moment to sigh,
We were two children together,
just my own baby and I!

HER NEW SONG

Dear Lord, my heart was but a willful thing,
Strong in its strength and ever on the wing:
It needed mastership, and Thou hast claimed it,
It needed taming, and Thy hand has tamed it.

Now, gentle, peaceful, harmless as a dove,
It lives as erst it lived its life, in love;
Love to all living things that Thou has made;
A love that is all sunshine without shade.

Thy fair, green earth is dotted as with flowers,
With little human souls, and blissful hours
I spend in blessed ministries to them.
Ah, many a flower I gather, many a gem!

And I have Thee! No battle's rude affray
Can ever tear Thee from my heart away;
And the cold hand that stole my boy from me,
Can never lay a claiming touch on Thee!

And so my life goes on, and to some eyes
Flinty and lonely all my pathway lies;
But Thou, who taking much, so much hast given,
Hast granted me the very peace of Heaven.

Through loss I passed to gain! Through death to life!
I kiss the rod that smote the youthful wife,
And love Him best who took away the boy,
And woke the mother from her dream of joy.

My God, Thine eye, omniscient and divine,
Rests on no happier, gladder heart than mine;
Empty of all things else, what room for Thee,
Who hast been, art, and will be, All to me!

APPENDIX ONE

The following material was found as an appendix to the original edition of *Golden Hours* by Mrs. Prentiss. It is her tribute to a very special lady, Mrs. Julia B. Cady. After introducing the piece with a biographical sketch of the author, she includes the poem by Mrs. Cady, and then adds her response to the poem with her own verse.

"New Year Thoughts"
From "The Sabbath at Home"

Those who read the beautiful lines thus entitled in the January edition of this Magazine, will feel a touching and sacred interest is attached to them when they learn that the warm heart that dictated, and the hand that gave them language, then lay cold in death.

Their author, Mrs. Julia B. Cady, was young and happy; the joy and pride of a sweet, Christian home; a blessed wife and mother, with everything to attract her to this life. But her face was ever set right heavenward; and when, just as the old year was closing, the summons to come up higher reached her, she had nothing to do but to lay aside her earthly garments, and to go. She had lived for Christ: her time, her thoughts, her work were all for Him. She loved His poor for His sake, and gathered them about her, counseled them, prayed with them, found employment for them, made herself one with them. She loved to welcome friendless waifs, tossed upon the tide of this great sea of city life [in NY City], into hospitable shelter. She loved little children, and made their interests her own. She loved the Church of Christ, and, one sacramental season after another, saw those united to it whose feet she had guided there. In a word, she loved Christ, and walked with God in an unobtrusive and meek pathway, that has now led her straight to His eternal embrace.

And hardly had she gone hence, when, like a voice from the grave, there came to her astonished, weeping friends, who saw it now for the first time, this cheerful greeting to the New Year; precious words, reserved for their joy and solace when they should enter that year without her. Would there were more homes like hers! Would there were more souls as saintly, as rich in faith and love, as hers! Would that every one who reads this brief notice could face the unknown future with the calm confidence with which she confronted it!

One touching incident may, perhaps, be added. At the close of the funeral-services, two friends slipped privately back to the church to take one more look at the peaceful face. There she lay, amid an opulent, nay, a regal profusion of flowers, the gift of those who loved and honored her and hers; and a group of poor women and children hung around her coffin, giving all they had to give. It was a beautiful contrast, such as is rarely seen upon earth; the testimony of the rich and the testimony of the poor—the flowers of the one, and the tears of the other. How little she knew, when she asked the coming year what it had in store for her, that it had these flowers and these tears, and the "Well done, good and faithful servant! Enter into the joy of thy Lord!"

New Year Thoughts

Farewell, Old Year! The rustle of whose garment,
   Fragrant with memory, I still can hear:
For all thy tender kindness and thy bounty
   I drop my thankful tribute on thy bier.

What is in store for me, brave New Year, hidden
   Beneath thy glistening robe of ice and snows?
Are there sweet songs of birds, and breath of lilacs,
   And blushing blooms of June's scent-laden rose?

Are there cold winds and dropping leaves of autumn,
Heart-searching frosts, and storm-clouds black and drear?
Is there a rainbow spanning the dark heaven?
   Wilt thou not speak and tell me, glad New Year?

As silent art thou of the unknown future
   As if thy days were numbered with the dead;
Yet, as I enter thy wide-open portal,
   I cross thy threshold with glad hope, not dread.

To me no pain or fear or crushing sorrow
   Hast thou the power without *His* will to bring;
And so I fear thee not, O untried morrow!
   For well I know my *Father* is thy King.

If joy thou bringest, straight to God, the giver,
   My gratitude shall rise; for 'tis His gift:
If sorrow, still, 'mid waves of Grief's deep river,
   My trembling heart I'll to my Father lift.

If life's full cup shall be my happy portion,
   With thankful joy I'll drink the precious draught;
If death, my waiting soul across Life's ocean
   But little sooner to my home 'twill waft.

So hope-lit New Year, with thy joys uncertain,
   Whose unsolved mystery none may foretell,
I calmly trust my God to lift thy curtain:
   Safe in His love, for *me* 'twill all be well.

                  J.B. Cady

Reply of the New Year

What had I hidden for thee in my bosom,
   Thou fearless listener at my clos-ed door?
With what sweet songs was I prepared to greet thee?
   What were the fragrant flowers I held in store?

Was it the song of birds, the breath of lilacs,
   The blushing blooms of June's scent-laden rose,
The rainbow-hues of beauty and of promise,
   The cup that with life's gladness overflows?

Nay, thou beloved one! Songs of angel voices
   Are the sweet notes that waited for thine ear;
Immortal are the flowers my hands had gathered
   To deck thy pathway to the brave New Year.

Mine was the joy to clasp thy hand, and lead thee
   Into green pastures: guide thy willing feet,
That oft had strayed that way, to the full fountain,
   To crystal rivers, waters clear and sweet;

To see thee in the garments pure and spotless
   In which His loved ones are by Jesus dressed;
Behold thee take possession of the mansion
   Provided for the long-expected guest.

Farewell, thou missed and mourned! In those fair regions,
   Where now thou art at home, there are no years;
There are no pains, or fears, or crushing sorrows,
   No frosts, no storm clouds, no cold winds, no tears.

Thine is no doubtful path, no fate uncertain;
   For thee no anxious fear one heart may swell:
But tear-dimmed eyes pierce Death's transparent curtain,
   And see thee safe with Christ,—all well, all well!

Jan. 3, 1870

APPENDIX TWO

The following material is taken from *The Life and Letters of Elizabeth Prentiss* (released as *More Love to Thee,* by Calvary Press Publishing). It is believed that these poems and letters will help the reader to appreciate more fully the heart-hymns found within the book, *Golden Hours.* It gave much pleasure to go back over these pages in preparing this volume for the press.

Each piece shall be placed in the order it appears in *The Life and Letters...*

LAMENT OF THE LAST PEACH

Written in 1836 at the age of 18 - p. 23

In solemn silence here I live,
    A lone, deserted peach;
So high that none but birds and winds
    My quiet bough can reach.
And mournfully, and hopelessly,
    I think upon the past;
Upon my dear departed friends,
    And I, the last, the last.

My friends! oh, daily one by one
    I've seen them drop away;
Unheeding all the tears and prayers
    That vainly bade them stay.
And here I hang alone, alone,
    While life is fleeing fast;
And sadly sigh that I am left
    The last, the last, the last.

Farewell, then, thou my little world
My home upon the tree,
A sweet retreat, a quiet home
Thou mayst no longer be;
The willow trees stand weeping nigh,
The sky is overcast,
The autumn winds moan sadly by,
And say, the last—the last.

HOPE FOR A NEW YEAR

Written at the start of 1843 at the age of 22 - p. 76

With mingling hope and trust and fear
I bid thee welcome, untried year;
The paths before me pause to view;
Which shall I shun and which pursue?
I read my fate with serious eye;
I see dear hopes and treasures fly,
Behold thee on thy opening wing
Now grief, now joy, now sorrow bring.
God grant me grace my course to run
With one blest prayer—*His* will be done.

The next entry in the book is from nearly ten years later, the era referred to in the Preface as the commencement of the most important years of her life. She was now married to Rev. George Lewis Prentiss, pastor of the South Trinitarian Church in New Bedford, MA, and blessed with two children, and pregnant with a third. Her first born was a girl, named Annie, born in December of 1846; the second, a boy, named Eddy, born in October of 1848. The time frame is the winter and spring of 1851-52. It will be left to her husband and herself to describe what took place at this time.

In the month of November the diary shows that her watchful eye observed in Eddy signs of disease, which filled her with anxiety. Before the close of the year her worst fears began to be realized. She wrote, Dec. 31: "I am under a constant pressure of anxiety about Eddy. How little we know what the New Year will bring forth." Early in January, 1852, his symptoms assumed a fatal type, and on the 16th of the same month the beautiful boy was released from his sufferings, and found rest in the kingdom of heaven, that sweet home of the little children. A few extracts from Eddy's journal will tell the story of his last days:

On the 19th of December the Rev. Mr. Poor was here. On hearing of it, Eddy said he wanted to see him. As he took now so little interest in anything that would cost him an effort, I was surprised, but told Annie to lead him down to the parlor; on reaching it they found Mr. Poor not there, and they then went up to the study. I heard their father's joyous greeting as he opened his door for them, and how he welcomed Eddy, in particular, with a perfect shower of kisses and caresses. This was the last time the dear child's own feet ever took him there; but his father afterwards frequently carried him up in his arms and amused him with pictures, especially with what Eddy called the "bear books." One morning Ellen told him she was going to make a little pie for his dinner, but on his next appearance in the kitchen told him she had let it burn all up in the oven, and that she felt *dreadfully* about it. "Never mind, Ellie," said he, "mamma does not like to have me eat pie; but when I *get well* I shall have as many as I want."

On the 24th of December Mr. Stearns and Anna were here. I was out with the latter most of the day; on my return Eddy came to me with a little flag which his uncle had given him, and after they had left us he ran up and down with it, and as my eye followed him, I thought he looked happier and brighter and more like himself than I had seen him for a long time. He kept saying, "*Mr.* Stearns gave me this flag!" and then would correct himself and say, "I mean my *Uncle* Stearns." On this night he hung up his bag for his presents, and after going to bed, surveyed it with a chuckle of pleasure peculiar to him, and finally fell asleep in this happy mood. I took great delight in arranging his and Annie's presents, and getting them safely into their bags. He enjoyed Christmas as much as I had reason to expect he would, in his state of health, and was busy among his new playthings all day. He had taken a fancy within a few weeks to kneel at family prayers with me at my chair, and would throw one little arm round my neck, while with the other hand he so prettily and seriously covered his eyes. As their heads touched my face as they knelt, I observed that Eddy's felt hot when compared with Annie's; just enough so to increase my uneasiness. On entering the nursery on New Year's morning, I was struck with his appearance as he lay in bed; his face being spotted all over. On asking Margaret about it, she said he had been crying, and that this occasioned the spots. This did not seem probable to me, for I had never seen anything of this kind on his face before. How little I knew that these were the last tears my darling would ever shed.

On Sunday morning, January 4, not being able to come himself, Dr. Buck sent Dr. Watson in his place. I told Dr. W. that I thought Eddy had water on the brain; he said it was not so, and ordered nothing but a warm bath. On Thursday, January 8, while Margaret was at dinner, I knelt by the side of the cradle, rocking it very gently, and he asked me to tell him a story. I asked what about, and he said, "A little boy," on which I said something like this: "Mamma knows a dear little boy who was very sick. His head ached and he felt sick all over. God said, I must let that little lamb come into my fold; then his head will never ache again, and he will be a very happy little lamb." I used the words little lamb because he was so fond of them. Often he would run to his nurse with his face full of animation and say, "Marget! Mamma says I am her little lamb!" While I was telling him this story his eyes were fixed intelligently on my face. I then said, "Would you like to know the name of this boy?" With eagerness he said, "Yes, yes, mamma!" Taking his dear little hand in mine, and kissing it, I said, "It was Eddy." Just then his nurse came in and his attention was diverted, so I said no more.

On Sunday, January 11, at noon, while they were all at dinner, I was left alone with my darling for a few moments, and could not help kissing his unconscious lips. To my utter amazement he looked up and plainly recognized me and warmly returned my kiss. Then he said feebly, but distinctly twice, "I want some meat and potato." I do not think I should have been more delighted if he had risen from the dead, once more to recognize me. Oh, it was *such* a comfort to have one more kiss, and to be able to gratify one more wish!

On Friday, January 16th, his little weary sighs became more profound, and, as the day advanced, more like groans; but appeared to indicate extreme fatigue, rather than severe pain. Towards night his breathing became quick and laborious, and between seven and eight slight spasms agitated his little feeble frame. He uttered cries of distress for a few minutes, when they ceased, and his loving and gentle spirit ascended to that world where thousands of holy children and the blessed company of angels and our blessed Lord Jesus, I doubt not, joyfully welcomed him. Now we were able to say, *It is well with the child.*

"Oh," said the gardener, as he passed down the garden-walk, "who plucked that flower? Who gathered that plant?" His fellow-servants answered, "The MASTER!" And the gardener held his peace.

The feelings of the mother's heart on Friday found vent in some lines entitled *To My Dying Eddy, January 16th.* Here are two stanzas :

> Blest child! dear child! For thee is Jesus calling;
>   And of our household thee—and only thee!
> Oh, hasten hence! to His embraces hasten!
>   Sweet shall thy rest and safe thy shelter be.
>
> Thou who unguarded ne'er hast left our threshold,
>   Alone must venture now an unknown way;
> Yet, fear not! Footprints of an Infant Holy
>   Lie on thy path. Thou canst not go astray.

In a letter to her friend Mrs. Allen, of New Bedford, dated January 28, she writes :

"During our dear little Eddy's illness we were surrounded with kind friends, and many prayers were offered for us and for him. Nothing that could alleviate our affliction was left undone or unthought of, and we feel that it would be most unchristian and ungrateful in us to even wonder at that Divine will which has bereaved us of our only boy; the light and sunshine of our household. We miss him *sadly*. I need not explain to you, who know all about it, *how* sadly; but we rejoice that he has got away from this troublous life, and that we have had the privilege of giving so dear a child to God. When he was well he was one of the happiest creatures I ever saw, and I am sure he is well now, and that he is as happy as his joyous nature makes him susceptible of becoming. God has been most merciful to us in this affliction, and, if a bereaved, we are still a *happy* household and full of thanksgiving. Give my love to both the children and tell them they must not forget us, and when they think and talk of their dear brother and sisters in heaven, they must sometimes think of the little Eddy who is there too."

The shock of Eddy's death proved almost too much for Mrs. Prentiss' enfeebled frame. She bore it, however, with sweet submission, and on the 17th of the following April her sorrow was changed to joy, and Eddy's empty place filled, as she thought, by the birth of Elizabeth, her third child, a picture of infantine health and beauty. But, although the child seemed perfectly well, the mother herself was brought to the verge of the grave. For a week or two her life wavered in the balance, and she was quite in the mood to follow Eddy to the better country. Her husband, recording a "long and most interesting conversation" with her on Sabbath evening, May 2nd, speaks of the "depth and tenderness of her religious feelings, of her sense of sin and of the grace and glory of the Savior," and then adds, "Her old Richmond (VA) exercises seem of late to have returned with their former strength and beauty increased many-fold." On the 14th of May she was able to write in pencil these lines to her sister, Mrs. Louisa Hopkins:

"I little thought that I should ever write to you again, but I have been brought through a great deal, and now have reason to expect to get well. I never knew how much I loved you till I gave up all hope of ever seeing you again, and I have not strength yet to tell you all about it. Poor George has suffered much. I hope all will be blessed to him and to me. I am still confined to bed. The doctor thinks there may be an abscess near the hip-joint, and, till that is cured, I can neither lie straight in bed or stand on my feet or ride out. Everybody is kind. Our cup has run over. It is a sore trial not to be allowed to nurse baby. She is kept in another room. I only see her once a day. She begins to smile, and is very bright-eyed. I hope your journey will do you good. If you can, do write a few lines, not more. But, good-by."

Hardly had she penned these lines, when, like a thunderbolt from a clear sky, another stunning blow fell upon her. On the 19th of May, after an illness of a few hours, Bessie, too, was folded forever in the arms of the Good Shepherd. Here is the mother's own story of her loss :

"Our darling Eddy died on the 16th of January. The baby he had so often spoken of was born on the 17th of April. I was too feeble to have any care of her. Never had her in my arms but twice; once the day before she died and once while she was dying. I never saw her little feet. She was a beautiful little creature, with a great quantity of dark hair and very dark blue eyes. The nurse had to keep her in another room on account of my illness. When she was a month old she brought her to me one afternoon. "This child is perfectly beautiful," said she; "tomorrow I mean to dress her up and have her likeness taken." I asked her to get me up in bed and let me take her a minute. She objected, and I urged her a good deal, till at last she consented. The moment I took her I was struck by her unearthly, absolutely angelic expression; and, not having strength enough to help it, burst out crying bitterly, and cried all the afternoon while I was struggling to give her up.

Her father was at Newark. When he came home at dark I told him I was sure that baby was going to die. He laughed at me, said my weak health made me fancy it, and asked the nurse if the child was not well. She said she was perfectly well. My presentiment remained, however, in full force, and the first thing next morning I asked Margaret to go and see how baby was. She came back, saying, "She is very well. She lies there on the bed scolding to herself." I cried out to have her instantly brought to me. She refused, saying the nurse would be displeased. But my anxieties were excited by the use of the word "scolding," as I knew no baby a month old did anything of that sort, and insisted on its being brought to me. The instant I touched it I felt its head to be of a burning heat, and sent for the nurse at once. When she came, I said, "This child is *very sick.*" "Yes," she said, "but I wanted you to have your breakfast first. At one o'clock in the night I found a little swelling. I do not know what it is, but the child is certainly very sick." On examination I knew it was erysipelas ['a disease known as St. Anthony's fire', ed.]. "Don't say that," said the nurse, and burst into tears. I made them get me up and partly dress me, as I was so excited I could not stay in bed.

Dr. Buck came at ten o'clock; he expressed no anxiety, but prescribed for her and George went out to get what he ordered. The nurse brought her to me at eleven o'clock and begged me to observe that the spot had turned black. I knew at once that this was fearful, fatal disease, and entreated George to go and tell the doctor. He went to please me, though he saw no need of it, and gave the wrong message to the doctor, to the effect that the swelling was increasing, to which the doctor replied that it naturally would do so. The little creature, whose moans Margaret had termed scolding, now was heard all over that floor; every breath a moan that tore my heart in pieces. I begged to have her brought to me but the nurse sent word she was too sick to be moved. I then begged the nurse to come and tell me exactly what she thought of her, but she said she could not leave her. I then crawled on my hands and knees into the room, being unable then and for a long time after to bear my own weight.

What a scene our nursery presented! Everything upset and tossed about, medicines here and there on the floor, a fire like a fiery furnace, and Miss H. sitting hopelessly and with falling tears with the baby on a pillow in her lap; all its boasted beauty gone forever. The sight was appalling and its moans heart-rending. George came and got me back to my sofa and said he felt as if he should jump out of the window every time he heard that dreadful sound. He had to go out and made me promise not to try to go to the nursery till his return. I foolishly promised. Mrs. White called, and I told her I was going to lose my baby; she was very kind and went in to see it but I believe expressed no opinion as to its state. But she repeated an expression which I repeated to myself many times that day, and have repeated thousands of times since-
"God never makes a mistake."

Margaret went soon after she left to see how the poor little creature was, and did not come back. Hour after hour passed and no one came. I lay racked with cruel torture, bitterly regretting my promise to George, listening to those moans till I was nearly wild. Then in a frenzy of despair I pulled myself over to my bureau, where I had arranged the dainty little garments my darling was to wear, and which I had promised myself so much pleasure in seeing her wear. I took out everything she would need for her burial, with a sort of wild pleasure in doing for her one little service, where I had hoped before to render so many. She it was whom we expected to fill our lost Eddy's vacant place; we thought we had

had our sorrow and that now our joy had come. As I lay back exhausted, with these garments on my breast, Louisa Shipman opened the door. One glance at my piteous face, for oh, how glad I was to see her! made her burst into tears before she knew what she was crying for.

"Oh, go bring me news from my poor dying baby!" I almost screamed, as she approached me. "And see, here are her grave-clothes." "Oh, Lizzy, have you gone crazy?" cried she, with a fresh burst of tears. I besought her to go, told her how my promise bound me, made her listen to those terrible sounds which two doors could not shut out. As she left the room she met Dr. B. and they went to the nursery together. She soon came back, quiet and composed, but very sorrowful. "Yes, she is dying," said she, "the doctor says so; she will not live an hour." At last we heard the sound of George's key. Louise ran to call him. I crawled once more to the nursery, and snatched my baby in fierce triumph from the nurse. At least once I would hold my child, and nobody should prevent me. George, pale as death, baptized her as I held her in my trembling arms; there were a few more of those terrible, never-to-be-forgotten sounds, and at seven o'clock we were once more left with only one child. A short, sharp conflict, and our baby was gone.

Dr. B. came in later and said the whole thing was to him like a thunderclap; as it was to her poor father. To me it followed closely on the presentiment that in some measure prepared me for it. Here I sit with empty hands. I have had the little coffin in my arms, but my baby's face could not be seen, so rudely had death marred it. Empty hands, empty hands, a worn-out, exhausted body, and unutterable longings to flee from a world that has had for me so many sharp experiences. God help me, my baby, my baby! God help me, my little lost Eddy!'"

But although the death of these two children tore with anguish the mother's heart, she made no show of grief, and to the eye of the world her life soon appeared to move on as aforetime. Never again, however, was it exactly the same life. She had entered into the fellowship of Christ's sufferings, and, the new experience wrought a great change in her whole being.

A part of the summer and the early autumn of 1852 were passed among kind friends at Newport, in Portland, and at the Ocean House on Cape Elizabeth. She returned much refreshed, and gave herself up cheerfully to her accustomed duties. But a cloud rested still upon her home, and at times the old grief came back again with renewed poignancy. Here are a few lines expressive of her feelings. They were written in pencil on a little scrap of paper :

MY NURSERY, 1852

I thought that prattling boys and girls
Would fill this empty room;
That my rich heart would gather flowers
From childhood's opening bloom.

One child and two green graves are mine,
This is God's gift to me;
A bleeding, fainting, broken heart-
This is my gift to Thee.

"TOO DEEP FOR TEARS"

Written on January 16, 1856, the fourth anniversary of Eddy's death, p. 143

Four years, four weary years, my child,
Four years ago to-night,
With parting cry of anguish wild
They spirit took its flight; ah me!
Took its eternal flight.

And in that hour of mortal strife
I thought I felt the throe,
The birth-pang of a grief, whose life
Must soothe my tearless woe, must soothe
And ease me of my woe.

Yet folded far through all these years,
Folded from mortal eyes,
Lying also "too deep for tears,"
Unborn, unborn it lies, within
My heart of heart it lies.

My sinless child! Upon thy knees
Before the Master pray;
Methinks thy infant hands might seize
And shed upon my way sweet peace;
Sweet peace upon my way.

THE CORNERSTONE
Written in November 1863 as the cornerstone was laid
for the Church of the Covenant in New York City -p. 216

A temple, Lord, we raise;
Let all its walls be praise
    To Thee alone.
Draw nigh, O Christ we pray,
To lead us on our way,
And be Thou, now and aye,
    Our cornerstone.

In humble faith arrayed,
We these foundations laid
    In war's dark day.
Oppression's reign o'erthrown,
Sweet peace once more our own,
Do Thou the topmost stone
    Securely lay.

And when each earth-built wall
Crumbling to dust shall fall,
    Our work still own.
Be to each faithful heart
That here hath wrought its part,
What in Thy Church Thou art—
    The Cornerstone.

A SIMPLE LULLABY

From Dorset, VT, p. 250

I know not the way I am going
But well do I know my Guide!
With a childlike trust I give my hand,
To the mighty Friend at my side.

The only thing that I say to Him
As He takes it, is, "Hold fast,
Suffer me not to lose my way,
And bring me home at last!"

REFLECTION UPON CHANGING HOMES

Written upon going to summer home in Dorset, June 1870, p. 307

Once more I change my home, once more begin
  Life in this rural stillness and repose;
But I have brought with me my heart of sin,
  And sin nor quiet nor cessation knows.

Ah, when I make the final, blessed change,
  I shall leave that behind, shall throw aside
Earth's soiled and soiling garments, and shall range
  Through purer regions like a youthful bride.

Thrice welcome be that day! Do thou, meanwhile,
  My soul, sit ready, unencumbered wait;
The Master bides thy coming, and His smile
  Shall bid thee welcome at the golden gate.

REFLECTING ON THE INFLUENCE OF FENELON

-found after her death as a tribute to Francis Fenelon (1651-1715),
whose writings were helpful to her in walking with her Lord, p. 321

Oh wise and thoughtful words! Oh counsel sweet,
Guide in my wanderings, spurs unto my feet,

How often you have met me on the way,
And turned me from the path that led astray;
Teaching that fault and folly, sin and fall,
Need not the weary pilgrim's heart appall:
Yea, more, instructing how to snatch the sting
From timid conscience, how to stretch the wing
From the low plane, the level dead of sin,
And mount immortal, mystic joys to win.
One hour with Jesus! How its peace outweighs
The ravishment of earthly love and praise;
How dearer far, emptied of self to lie
Low at His feet, and catch, perchance, His eye,
Alike content when He may give or take,
The sweet, the bitter, welcome for His sake!

In addition to Mrs. Prentiss' gift for writing verse, she was especially gifted and prolific in writing letters. It seems fitting to conclude this book with two letters that she wrote. The first to her dying sister-in-law, who was married to her brother Edward. They were life-long friends, and the husband was to be left to care for little children alone. The letter is dated October 28, 1867, and demonstrates uncommon sympathy:

"I have been so engrossed with sympathy for Edward and your children, that I have but just begun to realize that you are about entering on a state of felicity which ought, for the time, to make me forget them. Dear Nelly, *I congratulate you with all my heart.* Do not let the thought of what those who love you must suffer in your loss, diminish the peace and joy with which God now calls you to think only of Himself and the home He has prepared for you. Try to leave them to His kind, tender care. He loves them better than you do; He can be to them more than you have been; He will hear your prayers and all the prayers offered for them, and as one whom his mother comforteth, so will He comfort them. We, who shall be left here without you, can not conceive the joys on which you are to enter, but we know enough to go with you to the very gates of the city, longing to enter in with you to go out no more. All your tears will soon be wiped away; you will see the King in His beauty; you will see Christ your Redeemer and realize all He is and all He has done for you; and how many saints whom you have loved on earth will be standing ready to seize you by the hand and welcome you among them! As I think of these things my soul is in haste to be gone; I long to be set free from sin and self and to go to the fellowship of those who have done with them forever, and are perfect and entire, wanting nothing.

Dear Nelly, I pray that you may have as easy a journey homeward as your Father's love and compassion can make for you; but these sufferings at the worst can not last long, and they are only the messengers sent to loosen your last tie on earth, and conduct you to the sweetest rest. But I dare not write more lest I weary your poor worn frame with words. May the very God of peace be with you every moment, even unto the end, and keep your heart and mind stayed upon Him!"

The second was written just months later to her brother Edward, upon receiving the news that his son, Francis, had been taken from him, and gone to heaven with his mother. During the previous winter Edward and his youngest child had spent part of the winter in the Prentiss parsonage, and much of the book *Stepping Heavenward* was written with Francis in her arms. This letter exemplifies the desire she later expressed, "Much of my experience of life has cost me a great price, and I want to use it for the strengthening and comforting of others souls." Oh, how the Lord used her.

"Only this morning I was trying to invent some way of framing my little picture of Francis, so as to see it every day before my eyes. And now this evening's mail brings your letter, and I am trying to believe what it says is true. If grief and pain could comfort you, you would be comforted; we all loved Francis, and Annie has always said he was too lovely to live. How are you going to bear this new blow? My heart aches as it asks the question, aches and trembles for you. But perhaps you loved him so, that you will come to be willing to have him in his dear mother's safe keeping; will bear your own pain in future because through your anguish your lamb is sheltered forever, to know no more pain, to suffer no more for lack of womanly care, and is already developing into the rare character which made him so precious to you. Oh do try to rejoice for *him* while you can not but mourn for yourself. At the longest you will not have long to suffer; we are a short-lived race.

But while I write I feel that I want some one to speak a comforting word to me; I too am bereaved in the death of this precious child, and my sympathy for you is in itself a pang. Dear little lamb! I can not realize that I shall never see that sweet face again in this world; but I shall see it in heaven. God bless and comfort you, my dear afflicted brother. I dare not weary you with words which all seem a mockery; I can only assure you of my tenderest love and sympathy, and that we all feel with and for you as only those can who know what this child was to you. I am going to bed with an aching heart, praying that light may spring out of this darkness."

Recommended Reading

For those who desire to read more about this remarkable lady from the past, the following books are highly recommended.

More Love to Thee: The Life and Letters of Elizabeth Prentiss
by George Lewis Prentiss -
This is a beautiful edition of the definitive biography of Mrs. Prentiss, written by her husband. It contains all you need to know about this gracious sufferer. Lengthy but worth the time and effort it takes to read.
ISBN: 1-879737-14-0
CALVARY PRESS, PO Box 805 - Amityville, NY 11701
  1-800-789-8175   -   www.calvarypress.com

Legacy of a Legend: Spiritual Treasure from the Heart of Edward Payson
by Edward Payson
Edward Payson (1783-1827) was the godly and gifted father of Mrs. Prentiss. If you have appreciated *Golden Hours* you will love *Legacy of a Legend*. He was her hero in the truest sense of that word. This book is an absolute treasure.
ISBN: 0-9710169-2-5
SOLID GROUND BOOKS, PO Box 660132 - Vestavia Hills, AL 35266
  205-978-9469 - solid-ground-books.com

LEGACY of a LEGEND

Spiritual Treasure from the Heart of Edward Payson

"Edward Payson's wisdom in this little book rivals that of Thomas Adam's *Private Thoughts of Religion* for profound experiential depth and warm piety. Nearly every paragraph shows the leading of the Spirit and the experience of a lifetime of ministry.

This treasure is a miniature yet veritable Reformed systematic theology applied to mind and soul. Here are 19th-century Puritan "uses" in poignant form. Buy and read this book slowly. Use it as a daily devotional. Meditate on small dosages. You will be well rewarded and concur that here is practical divinity in its purest form."   **Joel Beeke**

"It will always be true that the further preachers enter into true evangelical experience, and the more they know of the Spirit of Christ, the more will the elements of tenderness and love, doxology and praise enter into their ministries. Edward Payson entered deeply into this love, and reflected it to an eminent degree. More readers of Payson today would surely bring blessings to the churches."   **Iain Murray**

"The wisdom of Edward Payson transcends time and place. Through his writings, and the writings of his daughter Elizabeth Prentiss, his legacy reaches over the centuries and graces our generation."   **Susan Hunt**

"One of the most noteworthy differences between contemporary Evangelical preaching and that of previous centuries is the God-centered language and reflection of the former as opposed to the man-centeredness of the latter. But previous eras were rich in such theologians and preachers. And among them Edward Payson stands tall. His own evangelical experience and profound meditation on God's Word gave his preaching and writing an unction that even today can lead men and women to be taken up more and more with the glorious being that is the triune God. Highly recommended."   **Michael Haykin**

List price **$9.95**
Order from us at 205-978-9469
or from solid-ground-books@juno.com
Visit our web site at http://solid-ground-books.com

Mothers of the Wise and Good
by Jabez Burns

In 1846 Pastor Jabez Burns produced a volume that he hoped would encourage women joyfully to embrace their highest calling: MOTHERHOOD. This volume will touch the hearts of men and women alike, as it sets forth the powerful influence of a mother upon some of the best and brightest this world has ever known. Augustine, Jonathan Edwards, the Wesleys, John Newton, and many others are set forth as examples.

Elisabeth Elliot has said, "This is a fascinating catalogue of Mothers of the Wise and Good, like Augustine's mother who watered the ground with her tears until he turned to Christ."

Susan Hunt has added, "I have looked for a book like this for many years...a book that challenges women to higher principles. I knew deep in my heart that it had been written. My delight was multiplied when I discovered that it was written by a pastor... Every mother, grandmother and spiritual mother, in other words every woman, will find great help and hope in this book."

Nancy Wilson has stated, "One of the great helps to the modern church is the reprinting of old books by saints of a previous generation. This book has much to offer us in our day where motherhood is not given the honor it deserves."

List price **$10.95**
Order from us at 205-978-9469
or from solid-ground-books@juno.com
Visit our web site at http://solid-ground-books.com

A PASTOR'S

Sketches

by Ichabod Spencer

This remarkable book was first published in 1850 by the man known as "The Bunyan of Brooklyn." This is the first edition within the last 100 years. Within the first two months it has been sent to over 20 countries throughout the world. Several of the most respected men and women of our day have sent us words of commendation. Here are a few:

"A Pastor's Sketches is a sobering and challenging reminder that the Holy Spirit is the true agent of conversion. This book is urgently needed today when so much of our evangelism is patterned after current marketing methods. It has deeply convicted me to always seek to be in tune with the Holy Spirit as I minister to others." **Jerry Bridges**

"We live in a day when it is rare for people to speak about their souls. But in times of revival such as that in which Ichabod Spencer lived, there was so much of the Holy Spirit's work in evidence in men's lives that ministers needed to address the most searching questions to their hearers. Few did this so well as Dr. Spencer, whose *Sketches*, reprinted after a lapse of many years, are a veritable treasury of pastoral wisdom. They will amply repay careful reading by pastors and serious Christians in our day." **Maurice Roberts**

"Spencer is a master at flushing sinners out of hiding and directing them to Jesus Christ for salvation through Spirit-worked, simple faith." **Joel Beeke**

List price **$12.95**
Order from us at 205-978-9469
or from solid-ground-books@juno.com
Visit our web site at http://solid-ground-books.com

SOLID GROUND CHRISTIAN BOOKS

Solid Ground Christian Books is a publishing venture that is determined to find and publish the very best books ever written. We are convinced that many of the best works of the past remain unknown and unavailable to the people of God. It is our goal to search out those works that God has been pleased to use in the past and bring them out once again before the people of God. We also hope to publish new works that will speak the timeless truth to the church and the world in the new century.

SGCB is committed to the doctrinal foundation of the great Reformation of the sixteenth century: *Grace Alone, Faith Alone, Christ Alone, Scripture Alone and God's Glory Alone.*

To assure that this publishing business remains on track we have established a Board of Pastoral Reference to oversee the direction of this work. These men have faithfully served the Lord for many years, and we delight to give their names.

Spreading the Fame of the Name of the Lord

Visit us at http://solid-ground-books.com
E-mail us at solid-ground-books@juno.com
Call us at 205-978-9469